"George Barna has been tracking the subtleties and nuances of American culture for more than three decades. In this book he paints a vivid but sometimes disturbing portrait of a nation in turmoil, using the most current national statistics as his color palate. His work is a call to action for Christ followers—people born for such a time as this who must understand the signs of the times in order to know what do. America is at a crossroads, and this book will help us navigate the future with greater confidence, wisdom, and authority."

Mark Batterson, *New York Times* bestselling author of *The Circle Maker,* lead pastor, National Community Church

"The only way to make the best decisions for your future is to understand the trends of the present. George Barna has summarized an enormous amount of data about Christianity and America that lays out all the important realities, positive and negative. *America at the Crossroads* is clear, practical, and ultimately hopeful. You owe it to yourself, your family, and your future to read this book."

Dr. John Townsend, *New York Times* bestselling author, leadership consultant, and psychologist

"*America at the Crossroads* is more than just a valuable and reliable collection of facts from Barna. It offers a panoramic view of the progressive collapse of American society while Christians stand by and watch with seeming indifference. His book provides a necessary prescription focusing on defining a clear vision, restoring a biblical worldview, and embracing personal brokenness before God. How could America go wrong with such a strategy for the future? Given the diagnosis laid out in this book, *Crossroads* provides a wise and much-needed action plan for reviving America."

David Barton, historian, bestselling author, and founder of WallBuilders

"It's no news flash that American culture and values have undergone massive and unprecedented changes. In *America at the Crossroads*,

George Barna dissects these major transformational changes and explores where we're likely headed next. Frankly, it doesn't matter whether we agree with all of his interpretations or prescriptions for turning the ship around. What matters most is that we get our heads out of the sand and honestly grapple with the hard facts and data he presents, because how we respond will shape the future of the church and American society as we know it."

Larry Osborne, author and pastor, North Coast Church

"A fascinating look at where we are and where we are going in America. George goes inside and outside the church to give the reader a comprehensive study on what makes our country tick and what could be her demise should we not reverse our course. We don't need any more ignorant Christians, and George has done his part to make sure we don't have any."

Tim Wildmon, president, American Family Association

"Some of us remember the old E. F. Hutton commercials: 'When E. F. Hutton speaks, people listen.' I hardly need to say this, but 'when George Barna writes, wise people read it!' I have no idea how many times I have quoted George Barna. Some contend he is the most quoted Christian in the nation. Get the book. Don't put it on a shelf. Read it. Mark it up. Memorize the key pieces of information that can equip you to give perspective on contemporary culture. I will. When George writes, I read."

Dr. Jim Garlow, senior pastor, Skyline Church

AMERICA
AT THE
CROSSROADS

AMERICA
AT THE
CROSSROADS

Explosive Trends Shaping America's Future
and What You Can Do about It

GEORGE BARNA

BakerBooks
a division of Baker Publishing Group
Grand Rapids, Michigan

© 2016 by George Barna

Published by Baker Books
a division of Baker Publishing Group
PO Box 6287, Grand Rapids, MI 49516-6287
www.bakerbooks.com

Paper edition published 2018
ISBN 978-0-8010-7585-8

Printed in the United States of America

The Library of Congress has cataloged the original edition as follows:
Names: Barna, George, author.
Title: America at the crossroads : explosive trends shaping America's future and what you can
    do about it / George Barna.
Description: Grand Rapids : Baker Books, 2016. | Includes bibliographical references.
Identifiers: LCCN 2016013300 | ISBN 9780801008313 (cloth)
Subjects: LCSH: Christianity—United States. | United States—Church history—21st century. |
    Christianity and culture—United States. | United States—Social conditions—21st century
Classification: LCC BR515 .B43 2016 | DDC 277.3—dc23
LC record available at https://lccn.loc.gov/2016013300

Scripture quotations are from the *Holy Bible*, New Living Translation, copyright © 1996, 2004, 2015 by Tyndale House Foundation. Used by permission of Tyndale House Publishers, Inc., Carol Stream, Illinois 60188. All rights reserved.

The author is represented by The FEDD Agency, Inc.

18 19 20 21 22 23 24   7 6 5 4 3 2 1

In keeping with biblical principles of creation stewardship, Baker Publishing Group advocates the responsible use of our natural resources. As a member of the Green Press Initiative, our company uses recycled paper when possible. The text paper of this book is composed in part of post-consumer waste.

CONTENTS

7

INTRODUCTION

Dickens's famous opening to *A Tale of Two Cities* offers an intriguing juxtaposition of the good and the bad: "It was the best of times, it was the worst of times . . ."

Despite the relative freedom and comfort that most Americans experience these days, surprisingly few would contend that they are living in the best of times. Millions of people would submit that these may well be the worst of times for a nation that has been extraordinarily blessed for more than a quarter of a millennium.

From the most hardened social critic to the most optimistic church lady, Americans recognize that they are living in dangerous and bewildering times. The evidence is everywhere, and it is undeniable. The gulf in perceptions and probable responses between elected officials and those who elected them is wider than at any previous time in memory. The possibility of terrorism striking near home has created substantial—and increasing—anxiety. Fewer American parents than at any time since scientific polling began believe their children will have a better life than they did. Violent crimes have become commonplace, while confidence in the police has plummeted. Distrust of government, social institutions, and businesses is at record-setting levels. People's sense of victimization, powerlessness, and social detachment is unprecedented. Climate change and other environmental challenges baffle people and add to their impression that the world is out of control. The nuclear armament of America-hating nations like Iran, Russia, and North Korea adds to the public's sense of fear. Religion has shifted from providing a sense of peace, purpose, and order to becoming a source of division and confusion.

As the nation's leaders try to make sense of the turbulence and chart a course forward, the United States is mired in an uncomfortable transitional era. Nobody knows how long the transition will last or exactly what the next era will be like because the country is still immersed in an internal battle to define the new America. Nations tend to change incrementally, but some of those increments have a shorter shelf life than others. It may be that the new era will be upon us faster than many expected.

This is a book designed to help you understand some of the key hinge points in that transition, what kind of nation the new era will likely bring about, and how you can influence that outcome.

Why Pay Attention to Trends?

America has become a culture that seems more interested in being "in the moment" than one that focuses on understanding the connections between past, present, and future, and how people's choices can and should influence the future. While being in the moment may be the flavor of the month, it may not advance the country's long-term interests.

The very concept of being "in the moment" is drawn from the Buddhist philosophy of mindfulness. That concept promotes awareness of what is happening in the here and now, overcoming the natural human tendency to default to living in accordance with habits and routines that can deaden our senses and block our ability to be thoroughly alive to every experience. Being more fully present as we go through our day is a way of experiencing reality to its utmost potential.

It's not necessarily wrong to live completely in the moment, especially if the alternative is remaining oblivious to the important facets of reality or operating with a dulled capacity. However, many people have run with the concept to the extent that they believe living in the moment is all there is, severing any ties between what happens in this moment and what will take place in the moments (and days, weeks, months, years) to come as a result of their immediate decisions. One can certainly become too obsessed with the future, investing too much time and energy into simply daydreaming or compulsively preparing for what is to come. The ideal is to seek a balance between grasping the historical realities that brought us to this moment, experiencing what is taking place now as fully as we can, and preparing to build a bridge from the past and present to a desired future.

That's where this book comes into play. Even a cursory understanding of cultural trends and patterns can help intentionally build a better bridge to an optimal future.

Another way of seeing the value of trend tracking is to realize that the future doesn't just happen; it is created by people committed to envisioning and facilitating specific outcomes in society. To have that kind of impact on the future, we have to understand where things are, glean lessons from the past, and then ascertain what it will take to generate a particular outcome or set of circumstances. The alternative is to let others create our future for us, rendering us victims of the future instead of shapers of tomorrow.

And if you are a Christian, *discovering and understanding cultural trends is both an assignment and a gift from God*. Consider some of the Bible passages that exhort us to discern what is happening around us so that we can be better stewards of the resources and opportunities God has entrusted to us.

1 Chronicles 12:32

The men of Issachar were effective leaders, and the other tribes of Israel sought their advice because those men "understood the signs of the times and knew the best course for Israel to take." Historical documents help us understand that they were religious scholars who spent time studying both sacred literature and cultural teachings. Their purpose was the same as ours should be in examining trends: to become aware and then prepared to handle likely conditions. *The key is not to simply know what is coming but to determine how to most intelligently and strategically respond to emerging circumstances.* That is true wisdom.

Matthew 16:1–3

Jesus noted that the religious leaders gathered data to forecast the weather but failed to gather data about something more important: what was likely to happen in their society. He scolded them for their inability to "interpret the signs of the times," intimating that being equipped to handle coming events was desirable. Jesus was alluding to His own resurrection and the coming of the kingdom of God. Among the principles we might draw from His statement, though, are that we should read the signs provided by God rather than waiting until we witness the sign of our choosing and recognize that even though such signs come in many forms—from the supernatural to the mundane—they are all significant and valuable.

Genesis 49:1–28

As Jacob prepared to die, he gathered his sons to give them his final words. He could have said anything at all but chose to tell them what would happen to them in the future, based on their established patterns of behavior he had observed. The knowledge Jacob passed along to each of his sons, whether an uplifting praise or a stinging rebuke, is described in the Scriptures as a blessing. By recognizing that the future is an extension of the past, he helped his progeny prepare for what was headed their way.

What Are Trends?

Sometimes the idea of trends takes on a mystique. But trends are simply patterns of thought and behavior that provide insight into the lives of people and their society. Trend tracking is nothing magical. It is simply the process of knowing what patterns of thought and behavior are important to follow, gathering relevant and reliable data about those factors, properly interpreting the information, and projecting what those thoughts and behaviors are likely to be in the future given the stability and transitions evident in the other important factors that concurrently influence a culture.

Hmm, maybe it's not such an easy or straightforward science after all. A bit of sociological art is surely involved in the process. Straight-line projections provide the simplest forecasts but they are rarely accurate. Life is a series of twists and turns, some we expect and some we do not, which makes trend tracking both more involved and challenging but also more interesting. In reflecting on the individuals and organizations that have historically done a laudable job of addressing emerging and shifting trends, I've concluded that adeptly tracking societal trends hinges on the realization that the future will not simply be more of the same. Effective trend estimation requires the ability to discern how a particular path may be altered by interference caused by unusual shifts in a plethora of related factors. The best trend trackers use multiple sources of relatively reliable data and then add a touch of professional instinct to guide their work.

But if you take a moment to consider the value of accurate trend tracking, you might begin to see the tremendous advantage provided by a more refined sense of the likely future. Knowledge about trends is not so much about amazing people with your predictions as it is about reading the signs of the times so as to live a more productive and impactful life. If you can interpret the signs appropriately, then you may gain multiple benefits, such as:

13

- assessing assumptions, knowing that assumptions are often misleading and dangerous
- identifying opportunities and obstacles, enabling you to prepare accordingly
- explaining cultural realities, and thus providing a chance to make the most of those realities due to such insight and understanding
- planning wisely, using your limited parcel of resources to their greatest effect

Such outcomes highlight the difference between tracking trends and promoting fads. Often, fads are the more interesting of the two—and they are certainly the less significant and enduring. Although some people use the terms fad and trend interchangeably, the two are quite different. *Fads* are characterized by short-lived, intense acceptance by a limited number of people. Fads gain their moment in the spotlight through concentrated media attention, suggesting that the behavior or item has widespread support or appeal. However, fads fade into obscurity after the craze has run its course. Examples of fads include things now viewed as silly, such as pet rocks, streaking, and flash mobs.

Change versus Transformation

It is also important to make the distinction between change and transformation. *Change* is short-term alteration that can occur rapidly—and can easily and quickly revert back to the original state of being or to yet a different point on the continuum. In contrast, *transformation* is a long-term shift that requires lots of time and resources before it takes root.

Most of the movement that reaps attention in our society is change, because it is easier to identify and moves rapidly enough to be newsworthy and exciting. Transformation moves at a more glacial pace; therefore, it is a tougher narrative to convey. However, transformation is the more significant of the two types of transition because by nature it redefines the culture. To describe this with an analogy pertaining to personal appearance, change is like switching brands of makeup, whereas transformation is like getting plastic surgery.

So, for example, the recent decline in national church attendance is a reflection of change, while the drop in the proportion of people who believe Jesus Christ has anything to do with people's eternal destiny is transformation. They both matter, but transformation has extensive ramifications and a dramatic impact on the very nature of society.

This book will focus more on the elements of transformation than on examples of mere change. While change is significant, transformation is the real deal. By the way, keep in mind that change is inevitable and common. In contrast, transformation is exceptional and occurs infrequently—but when it does, it carries with it historic realities.

Regardless, both change and transformation are reshaping the national character. Assuming things will remain as they have been is not only ignorant but also a recipe for irrelevance and ultimate defeat.

Is This a New Approach?

Depending on your age and awareness, you may know that the 1980s were a kind of heyday for trend tracking. Numerous bestselling books released during that decade and featured the prognostications of various self-proclaimed cultural prophets. As you might imagine, some of them were better than others.

John Naisbitt wrote the groundbreaking book *Megatrends* in which he used a variety of information sources that were available to everyone—such as newspaper and magazine articles, as well as television newscasts—to identify a small number of trends he believed would radically alter the way we lived. Faith Popcorn was another trend watcher and very adept self-marketer who wrote a book (*The Popcorn Report*) that laid out a variety of more complicated trends she believed would come to pass. Some more sophisticated research groups also produced trend reports and newsletters, ranging from the esteemed public opinion researchers at Yankelovich, Skelly and White (who published the *Yankelovich Monitor*, a sophisticated social-tracking report) to the work of various futurist organizations.

In fact, an entire industry was suddenly born out of the growing interest in the future and the trends shaping it, creating a number of people who called themselves futurists and who produced various media describing their projections and predictions. Fascinated with the coming of the new millennium and armed with new tools (such as powerful computers and near-universal ownership of telephones, which allowed public opinion surveys to proliferate), the new breed of trend trackers made the most of their window of opportunity.

The 1990s and beyond, however, saw a diminished interest in trend tracking as the nation embraced a new worldview—postmodernism. (By the way, the widespread acceptance of postmodernism was a powerful trend that most of the prognosticators missed; they identified the symptoms but not the precipitating cause.) This new philosophy of life, an updated version of existentialism, placed a premium on experience, adventure, risk-taking, authenticity, emotional fulfillment, and spontaneity. Consequently, interest in endeavors such as planning and establishing efficient procedures held little appeal to the population. Trend tracking gave way to new interests.

The flagging public interest in forecasting the future, however, did not minimize the value of identifying trends—it only made the act of doing so less mainstream. A deeper analysis of what has happened since the shift shows that the organizations that have had to stay on the cutting edge of change have continued to utilize trend-tracking capabilities. Entities such as the military, the intelligence community, and many leading corporations have continuously and unapologetically invested resources in estimating what was coming down the pike. Through years of experience, those entities know that a critical dimension of effective leadership is anticipation and preparation.

The emergence of new technologies and technological applications has given new life to trend tracking. The current decade has ushered in the era of "Big Data"—the creation of massive data files on each person, built from a substantial number of data sources, combining every type of input imaginable to glean useful insights into people's thoughts and behavior. The mountains of data collected and analyzed by Big Data practitioners would cause a researcher armed only with rudimentary computer programs and computing power to go insane. But the extraordinary power of today's computing systems, using increasingly sophisticated software to crunch the data and make sense of patterns not discernible to the naked eye or the human brain, facilitates complex analyses and the development of clever communication strategies. The result is that many marketers and social scientists not only know more about us than we know about ourselves, but they also are able to develop solutions to needs and desires we don't even know we have or will have, long before we figure it out and search for those solutions.

Good Data, Bad Data

The Constitution of the United States boldly proclaims that all people are created equal. The same cannot be said for data. You would be shocked at how much of the data (and related interpretation) to which you are exposed is what might be labeled "bad data"—statistics that are either wrong, out of context, or misinterpreted. This has created a new skill that good researchers must possess: the ability to discern the good from the bad. The mere existence of a statistic does not make it valid. And despite the popularity of the huge volume of information introduced by the wizards of the Big Data movement, a greater quantity of bad data does not convert it into good data. Good researchers do not automatically assume that any piece of data is viable or accurate; they turn to various tests to ascertain the legitimacy and reliability of various bits of available information.

Here, for instance, are some of the principles that enable us to determine if specific facts or interpretations are trustworthy:

- Information that is descriptive but does not help explain or predict behavior is simply interesting noise. In other words, all information needs to pass the "so what?" test. Measures of attitudes, values, opinions, or behaviors that fail to shed light on how or why specific outcomes occur is, at best, simply entertainment and, at worst, a nuisance.

- Numerical data may all look the same, but they are not the same. Based on how the information was collected, why it was collected, when it was generated, and the various statistical treatments to which the information was subjected, the resulting data may or may not be sufficiently valid or accurate to justify consideration.

- The importance of having current, reliable, and accurate data cannot be overstated. Bad data leads to bad decisions. It is sometimes possible to mask how unreliable certain data are by providing them in massive quantities. Having a lot of statistical garbage does not change the fact that it is garbage, regardless of how much garbage you possess.

- Context is critical. No piece of information exists within a vacuum. Grasping the context of the information—both in terms of its genesis and its implications—is challenging but important.

With these principles in mind, know that the sources of information used in this book are intentionally limited. I firmly believe that most of the data to which you and I are exposed are garbage—more misleading and harmful rather than helpful. For instance, more than three thousand public opinion research companies exist in this country, but my experience with many of them has led me to be extremely careful about whose data I trust. I encourage you to also become a wise data consumer so you do not get misled by facts and figures that look professional but are not trustworthy.

The Content of This Book

We could study hundreds of cultural trends and trend dimensions in these pages. But in the interest of keeping things lively and interesting, if not comprehensive, the parameters of our evaluation are restricted to three significant areas: lifestyles and perspectives, faith and spirituality, and government and politics. That limits our scope of understanding to some degree, but by investigating these areas, we will get a solid handle on where things are today and where they may be tomorrow in American society. If you become interested enough to pursue trend tracking even further, additional sources of information are accessible. But this book should provide a broad-based, useful portrait of the recent past, the present, and my perception of our likely future.

Numerous areas of cultural development are fascinating but not germane to our discussion here. These include:

- new technologies (self-driving cars, for instance, are just around the corner)
- demographic shifts (e.g., the rapid expansion of the Asian-American population)
- consumption behavior (such as the adoption of Bitcoin and mobile payments)

Instead, we will concentrate on dimensions of American life that relate to the heartbeat of the culture and are more likely to define who Americans will be as a people and the implications of that national character.

Since this book is unique among the trend books I have seen, let me explain the format.

Research indicates that most people do not have or allow for prolonged periods of time for reading anymore. America also has been described as an ADD society—a people who have shorter attention spans and are more comfortable jumping from activity to activity without a felt need for completion. That is one of the reasons why book chapters, news and magazine articles, and many other media forms (think texting, Twitter, and Snapchat) are getting briefer. Even research reports are shorter and more direct than traditionally has been the case.

Consequently, my goal for the organization of this book is twofold. First, I want to provide information in bite-size pieces without compromising the quality of the information. Second, I want to divide the information into categories that help you more easily organize the information in your mind and thus be able to absorb a greater breadth and volume of information.

Each chapter is divided into three sections. The initial portion, labeled Summary, describes the recent past and current state of affairs related to the chapter's topic. Because society now seems to move in three- to five-year trending cycles, I have chosen not to give data comparisons that amount to ancient history. In most cases, the comparative data I will rely on go back as far as 1990, but rarely prior to that. The pace of change in America is so rapid, and the depth of change so substantial, that you can usually grasp the magnitude of change by looking back twenty-five years or less. In fact, comparing what is happening today with what took place in 1960—a time that is well within the memory of many of the people likely to read this book—is in many ways irrelevant. Americans have not lived in a cultural context that resembles 1960 for several decades, making data comparisons with that period an exercise in historical exegesis rather than cultural pertinence.

The second section of each chapter, called Key Facts, is a straightforward listing of some of the central bits of data related to the chapter's discussion. While the Summary contains a narrative that incorporates some facts and figures to make the case for where we are today, the Key Facts section bridges the opening and closing portions of each chapter with a quick and simple display of the statistics central to the argument.

The closing section of the chapter is titled Outlook and Interpretation. Whereas the first two portions provide an objective recitation of reliable information, the third section is my subjective assessment of what I think the data are telling us—the future outcomes that the trends and patterns previously described are leading me to expect. Also, some chapters include a graphic element to help you visualize the data—a chart or graph that communicates the information from a different angle.

You May Not Agree

I fully expect that you will disagree with my conclusions in portions of the Outlook and Interpretation sections. In my younger days, such disagreements would have frustrated me. These days I view them as a reasonable outcome and a positive indication that you are conscientiously reflecting upon the content! Please know I have come to the conclusions on these pages based on the data provided as well as a macro-level perspective on all the trends being explored in this book. I say that not to discourage you from challenging my conclusions but to diffuse possible concerns that you feel the data presented do not lead to the stated outcome. Thinking critically about the information presented is important to move beyond simply being informed toward making wise and strategic decisions based on what you know.

Let me also note that the final section—Standing at the Crossroads—provides some of the macro-level thinking that underlies much of this book. It is based not only on the data presented in these pages but also on reams of additional data that I analyze in my research for the nonprofit American Culture & Faith Institute (a division of United in Purpose) and for my own firm, Metaformation. This section is also a subjective perspective on the future of America. It is founded on a very specific point of view influenced heavily by my faith in Jesus Christ.

For purposes of full disclosure, understand that I believe America will be a better nation if its people live in harmony with the life principles God has provided in the Bible. I am not arguing for a theocracy or for Christianity to be instituted as the state-sanctioned religion of the land. I am, however, suggesting that when people embrace God's principles and hold themselves accountable to them, everyone is better off. I envision a country in which Christianity is respected and able to be practiced without government interference; the traditional family is unimpaired by the law when it reflects biblical values and behavior; success is defined according to spiritual rather than material outcomes; the Christian Church is vibrant and healthy and unapologetic for its beliefs and related behaviors; and our national values and objectives reflect those described in Scripture.

Again, you and I may have some divergent views, but a healthy and free society benefits from such exchanges. Respectful critical thinking that leads to sharper dialogue and superior decision-making will serve all of us well. My driving value in life is the desire to know and convey truth. It shapes everything I do in research, business, ministry, and writing, but I realize trend tracking is an art, leaving room for discussion, reconsideration, and even agreeing to disagree on some factors. Hopefully, our mutual efforts to lead America to a better future will also allow us to sharpen one another's abilities, insights, and choices.

The bottom line is that I hope this book will enlighten you, surprise you, affirm you, challenge you, and help you. People who succeed in life are inevitably those who anticipate rather than react. Tracking cultural trends is the process of anticipating what is coming down the road. May you see the changes coming before they happen and be ready to deal with them.

PART 1

FAITH AND SPIRITUALITY

1
RELIGIOUS
BELIEFS

Summary

Religious beliefs are the Rodney Dangerfield of cultural analysis: they get little attention and even less respect. Yet, those beliefs constitute the centerpiece of people's decision-making in virtually every aspect of life. What we believe about the existence and nature of God, the veracity and reliability of the Bible, the means to and nature of eternal salvation, the concepts of truth, love, forgiveness, power, purpose, and sin—these are the fundamental perspectives on which our moment-to-moment choices are based. The failure to grasp what is happening with people's core beliefs severely limits the ability to understand the present and future conditions of a society.

A careful study of Americans' core beliefs reveals a nation in transition, moving from a predominantly Judeo-Christian point of view to a mostly postmodern, secular worldview. The transition has been both rapid and monumental in its ramifications, as seen in the breathtakingly quick acceptance of same-sex marriage and the widespread acceptance of expanding government authority. Those who have strategically tracked the shift in our central faith tenets have seen the cultural earthquake coming for some time.

It is clear that the faith realm is in turmoil. In 2005, two-thirds of American adults said their religious faith was very important to them. Just ten years later that had slipped to only half. While millions of Americans contend, often defensively, that they are "spiritual but not religious," their notion of being spiritual is typically tied more to their sense of self-determination and spiritual independence than to a historic faith steeped in truth, tradition, or orthodoxy. In fact, the number of adults who label themselves "deeply spiritual" has declined by almost 40 percent since 2005.[1]

Nine out of ten adults believe in "God." However, only six out of ten believe in the God of the Christian Bible—a deity who is all-knowing, omnipresent, has unlimited power, created the universe, and rules that universe today and forever. Belief in such a God has dropped by seven percentage points in the past decade.[2]

Most Americans (78 percent) accept the idea that Jesus Christ was a real person,[3] but fewer than four out of ten believe that He was both human and divine and that He lived a sinless life on Earth. A growing proportion of Americans are uncertain about the nature and ministry of Jesus. Compared to a decade ago, fewer people have made a "personal commitment" to Jesus Christ that is important to them. Some have made that commitment to the person of Christ, while others have made it to the idea of a savior or spiritual protector. Combined, only six out of ten now say they have made such a commitment, down from nearly three-quarters of Americans just ten years ago. Further, fewer than half of all Americans (45 percent) contend that Jesus Christ is actually alive today.[4]

During the past decade, Americans have become more lukewarm about eternal salvation. While the same proportion of adults (three out of every ten) reject the idea that a good person can earn a place in Heaven, a larger and growing share of the public (about half) doesn't know what to think about what happens after they die. This rise in uncertainty corresponds to the decline in the percentage of born-again Christians who believe they have a responsibility to share the gospel with nonbelievers during the course of the year—a twelve-point decline in the last ten years. Meanwhile, the percentage of believers who have shared their faith with nonbelievers has dropped from two-thirds to less than one-half in the last decade.[5]

Perceptions about Satan are another point of theological murkiness for millions of Americans. Barely one-quarter of the public believes Satan is a living entity. A similar proportion believes Satan is merely a symbol of evil but not a living entity. The other half of the public is not sure what to make of the idea of the devil. Overall, Satan is not a being or a spiritual concept that most Americans take seriously.[6]

The Bible no longer holds the revered place in society that it once had. Most households (91 percent) still own one or more copies of the Bible, but barely one-third of all adults firmly believe that it is totally accurate in all of the principles it teaches. Not quite one-half of the public confidently embraces the view that the Bible contains everything you need to know to live a meaningful life.[7]

Overall, slightly more than one-half of the public believes the Bible is either the actual word of God, to be taken literally (22 percent), or the inspired and inerrant word of God, containing symbolism (33 percent). Almost one-half of the population (44 percent) contends that the Bible contains historical errors or personal interpretations that prevent it from being a trustworthy document. Some of the doubt about the Bible's reliability relates to the miracles it describes; just half of all adults believe they actually occurred.[8]

As for sacred literature, a majority of people aren't sure what to make of the documents relied on by the world's most popular religions. Most people lean toward believing that the Bible, Koran, and Book of Mormon are simply different expressions of the same spiritual truths. It is not surprising, then, that only one out of eight adults considers themselves to be "highly knowledgeable" about the content of the Bible.[9]

Key Facts

Spiritual Indicator	2005	2015
Self-description: deeply spiritual	58%	37%
"My religious faith is very important to me"	68	52
Have a personal responsibility to share religious beliefs with nonbelievers	34	25
God is the all-knowing, all-powerful creator of the universe who still rules it today	69	62
Bible is totally accurate in all of the principles it teaches	45	36
Bible is neither the actual nor inspired Word of God; it is written by men	22	30
Have made a personal commitment to Jesus Christ that is still important in my life today	72	60

Sources: OmniPoll™1-05, Barna Group, Ventura, CA, N=1,003, January 2005; OmniPoll™1-15, Barna Group, Ventura, CA, N=2,005, January 2015.

Adults Who Say Faith Is Their Highest Priority in Life

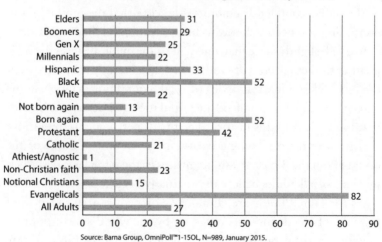

Elders	31
Boomers	29
Gen X	25
Millennials	22
Hispanic	33
Black	52
White	22
Not born again	13
Born again	52
Protestant	42
Catholic	21
Athiest/Agnostic	1
Non-Christian faith	23
Notional Christians	15
Evangelicals	82
All Adults	27

Source: Barna Group, OmniPoll™1-15OL, N=989, January 2015.

Outlook and Interpretation

Clearly, orthodox Christianity is much less popular in America today than it was just one decade ago. The continued questioning if not rejection of the Bible as a standard of truth has led tens of millions of people to adopt new morals, values, and behaviors. People are confused regarding what to believe and how to integrate their faith into the fabric of their lives, which is a testimony to the different voices and perspectives influencing their worldview.

Can you identify any nation in world history that abandoned biblical beliefs for a more secular worldview, only to quickly realize the error of its ways and return to biblically orthodox beliefs? Such transitions usually occur, if they happen at all, after a prolonged era of pain and decline. The United States is in the early stages of biblical abandonment and the consequent cultural decline. Increasing numbers of people are comfortable with faith as long as it provides the benefits they seek and is neither demanding nor constraining. This shift began tentatively more than four decades ago and has been gathering momentum ever since. Millennials, the generation whose choices will ultimately determine the nature of Christianity and the Church in America for several decades, appear poised to wholeheartedly support the shift away from biblical Christianity and toward new belief patterns.

The biblical warning that best captures the condition in America comes from the book of Judges, which tells us: "In those days Israel had no king; all the people did whatever seemed right in their own eyes" (17:9). Substitute "United States" for "Israel" and you have an accurate reflection of the present situation: a nation with no acknowledged King or deity, a nation in which its people have declared themselves in charge of their lives and destinies. Paul's warning that the world will enter a time when people will "no longer listen to sound and wholesome teaching" (2 Tim. 4:3) but instead will "follow their own desires and will look for teachers who will tell them whatever their itching ears want to hear" (v. 4) and "reject the truth and chase after myths" (v. 4) is an apt description of America at the start of the twenty-first century.

A fundamental principle of human behavior is that you do what you believe. The country's present situation suggests that Americans are on a course to engage in an increasing body of unbiblical behaviors without guilt or restraint. Almighty God can cause us to repent instantly should He so desire, but His preference is to give us the consequences of the exercise of our free will. It seems that we have a small window of opportunity to imagine what a twenty-first-century nation beholden to biblical principles might look like and how to foster such a transformation, but with each passing day the chance of successfully doing so seems to shrink.

2

RELIGIOUS BEHAVIOR

Summary

As noted in chapter 1, people do what they believe. Given that chapter's description of how Americans' beliefs are moving further from biblical Christianity, it is not surprising to find that people's religious behavior patterns are also becoming less orthodox.

The frequency of people's participation in every common religious activity—attending church services, reading the Bible, praying, volunteering at a church, joining a Sunday school class, participating in a small group—has significantly declined in the past decade. And the reduction of religious effort is not simply among the secular masses; the decline has been equally as sharp among the born-again segment.

The local church has certainly lost its place in the life routine of Americans. Long gone are the days when most people attended a church service each week. These days the turnout barely tops one-third of the population. This dramatic fall off in attendance has multiple causes. Research indicates that no single reason keeps most people away from churches.[1] The most common reasons include:

- doubting that the church has their best interests in mind
- not sensing the presence of God at the church
- busyness or work schedules that conflict with church activities
- the absence of children among young couples
- disinterest in or mistrust of the Bible
- a sense that the church's teachings or theology are restrictive, exclusive, stifling, shallow, or irrelevant
- attachment to relational networks that have no connection to churches or a common faith

Alternatives to the conventional church experience, such as house churches, experienced a dramatic increase a few years ago, but even that wave of enthusiasm has died down. House churches now attract about 4 percent of the population—although they are three times as popular among evangelicals (12 percent attend in a typical month).[2]

While some of the erosion of the public's church connection is attributable to the perception of dissatisfying church performance and the irrelevance of church teaching and activities to their personal needs, an infrequently discussed dimension of the shift may relate to adults' rising reliance on media and technology to deliver their God moments. Currently, 20 percent of all adults—and one-third of born-again adults—interact through social networks for a portion of their spiritual experience. Another 6 percent listen to Christian teaching and talk radio each week. A growing number of adults, reflecting 20 percent of all adults (and about twice as many born-again adults), use various forms of digital spiritual experience, other than social networks, to gather information, gain perspective, or engage with other believers about their faith. And the dominant force of media ministry, Christian television, continues to attract a substantial audience each week, estimated to be about one-fifth of all adults. Combine the audiences of these media and we're looking at an unduplicated proportion of almost half of the population gaining some level of spiritual nourishment and interaction from media sources. Add the spiritual content drawn from print media (e.g., books, magazines, newsletters), and the share of the market constitutes a majority of adults.[3] The large audience using media-based faith experiences is evidence of the fact that even though a conventional church experience may be losing its appeal to Americans, the Christian faith retains substantial appeal to a broad swath of the population.

One of the most alarming trends is the severe drop in the proportion of born-again Christians sharing the gospel with the nonbelievers. The ideal form of church growth, of course, is by attracting nonbelievers to follow Christ and become part of a community of faith. However, in just the last ten years, the share of believers expressing the gospel to non-Christians has plummeted from more than half (55 percent) to barely one-third (35 percent).[4] If the gospel remains a secret, it is virtually impossible for the Church to attract new adherents.

Although a majority of *evangelical* Christians are still involved in sharing their faith—and they appear to be the only subgroup of the nation's population in which a majority do so—they represent such a small proportion of the population (7 percent) that their potential reach is limited. The non-evangelical born-again segment, which outnumbers evangelicals by about a four-to-one ratio, typically does most of the gospel outreach in the United States. (FYI, a non-evangelical born-again Christian is someone who has confessed their sins and invited Jesus to be their Savior but does not embrace biblical positions related to some core elements of the Christian faith.) However, in the past decade, their engagement in interpersonal evangelism has plummeted from 52 percent to 34 percent. Several born-again segments are responsible for even larger shares of their members ceasing to share the gospel, as witnessed by a 36-point decline among born agains residing in the Northeast, a

33

32-point dive among nonwhites, a 29-point drop among Gen Xers, and a 28-point decrease among believers living in the South. In fact, perhaps the most surprising evangelistic shift of all is that men are now more likely to share the gospel than are women—the first time that pattern has been seen in more than thirty years of faith tracking by the Barna Group.

As alluded to in chapter 1, which describes people's loss of faith in the Bible's accuracy and reliability, behavioral measures reveal that Bible reading is considerably less common than it was a decade ago. In general, about four out of ten adults read God's Word at least once a week outside of church services, roughly one-quarter does so less than once a week but at least once a year, and the remaining one-third or so reads it less than once a year or never. In other words, people are more likely to watch TV, play games, listen to music, read for pleasure or news, evaluate their finances, listen to the radio, exercise—well, simply put, they're more likely to do any of more than two dozen leisure activities than to read the Bible. This dismissal of the Scriptures reflects people's priorities in a very tangible manner.[5]

Given the importance Americans attach to money, it is not surprising that people's giving to religious entities has also dropped precipitously in the last ten years. In 2014, nearly half of all adults (45 percent) gave no money to a church or other religious organization, a significant jump from the 36 percent who gave nothing in 2004. Among those who gave anything, the median total donations to religious organizations for the entire year was $500—just half the average cumulative donations provided in 2004. In addition, whereas a miniscule 5 percent of adults tithed their income to religious organizations and churches a decade ago, only half as many did so in 2014 (slightly more than 2 percent)—the lowest proportion of adults to do so in the twenty-plus years the Barna Group has been tracking tithing.[6]

Key Facts

- 20 percent of adults say they have read the Bible from start to finish; 36 percent of born-again Christian adults make that claim.[7]
- Only one-third (36 percent) believe churches are very committed to the respondent's best interests.[8]
- More than one-third of adults (36 percent) rarely or never read the Bible; 14 percent read it one to four times a year; 8 percent do so about once a month; three out of ten (29 percent) read it once a week; one in ten (11 percent) read it multiple times each week; and just 2 percent read the Bible every day.[9]
- Apart from a conventional Christian church setting, 4 percent of adults attend a house church—an independent church gathering that is not associated with a local church—indicating that house church growth has stalled. However, among evangelicals, the proportion participating in a house church has doubled from 6 percent to 12 percent during the past decade.[10]

Spiritual Indicator	All Adults		Born Again	
	2005	2015	2005	2015
During the past week: prayed to God	82%	75%	97%	95%
During the past week: attended a church service	45	36	65	56
During the past week: read from the Bible	45	33	67	59
During the past week: volunteered at a church	26	16	38	30
During the past week: participated in a small group/cell group	23	10	36	21
During the past week: attended an adult Sunday school or other Christian education class	20	12	36	25
During the past year: explained your religious beliefs to someone who had different beliefs, hoping they would accept Jesus Christ as their Savior	n/a	n/a	55*	35**

Sources: OmniPoll™1-05, Barna Group, Ventura, CA, N=1,003, January 2005; OmniPoll™1-15, Barna Group, Ventura, CA, N=2,005, January 2015; * OmniPoll™1-04, Barna Group, Ventura, CA, N=1,014, January 2004; ** OmniPoll™1-14, Barna Group, Ventura, CA, N=1,024, January 2014.

Religious Activities During a Typical Week

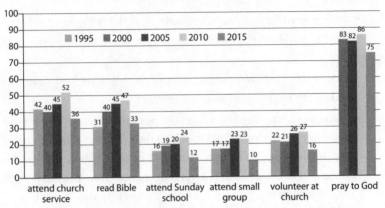

Sources: Barna Group, OmniPoll™1-15C, N=2,005, January 2015; OmniPoll™1-10, N=1,005, January 2010; OmniPoll™1-05, N=1,003, January 2005; OmniPoll™1-00, N=1,002, January 2000; OmniPoll™1-95, N=1,006, January 1995.

Outlook and Interpretation

Several of the findings described in this chapter provide ominous warnings about the Church's future in America. Not the least of those is the precipitous drop in the number of Christ followers who are sharing the gospel. Evangelism is, after all, the oxygen of Christianity. America's emerging culture, driven by its politically correct attitudes and a passion for silencing Christianity displayed by numerous liberal power brokers, has sucked the spiritual oxygen out of our society. Are Christians willing to do what it takes to reverse this trend? The smart money says the answer is "no" for the foreseeable future. It is more likely that growing numbers of believers will acquiesce to pressure to keep their beliefs private.

Engagement in church life is clearly on a downward slope as well. It is more likely that individualized forms of faith activity will grow, especially through various forms of media and technology, than return to corporate religious activity in local church settings.

Americans' relationship with the Bible is complex. Despite its hallowed past and historical role as a cornerstone for the nation, people have been slowly weaning themselves from it over the past quarter century, though they are not likely to abandon it altogether. It is more likely that Americans will move toward an 80/20 split: roughly 20 percent of the adult public will regularly read and revere the Bible and the other 80 percent will be aware of but emotionally, spiritually, and intellectually distant from it. One of the more onerous results of this wayward course is that the already dangerously low proportion of people who possess a biblical worldview will decline.

Because faith is as much a matter of the heart as of the head, it is important to consider what is likely to happen with people's financial support of the Christian faith in its various dimensions. The shifting attitudes of young Americans make it likely that parachurch organizations focused on helping the poor and the persecuted will continue to raise substantial amounts of money for their efforts. Churches, however, seem poised to be the recipients of diminished levels of giving. It is not a good time to think about seeking a paid job with churches.

3
THE
UNCHURCHED

Summary

Being a social scientist in the 1950s must have been rather boring. Year after year, key indicators stayed the same. A percentage point up on this measure, maybe two points down on that one. Consistency was the name of the game. It was like being a weather forecaster in Southern California who could thoughtlessly predict "sunny, warm, a slight breeze from the ocean, no rain in sight" and be right 95 percent of the time.

Then the Baby Boomers came of age and all bets were off. Without warning, religion became the only aspect of social change that lagged. That dimension provided a modicum of stability—for a while.

Perhaps it was inevitable that the sinners and the saints eventually demanded their day in the statistical spotlight. That day is here, as the faith arena is now where the action is. Church attendance, long one of the measures that shifted less often than the direction of Earth's rotation, is suddenly in play. The march toward total personal independence has heavily influenced the American population, causing people to view spirituality as a private matter to be pursued on one's own terms, in one's own timing. Attending church services has been one of the casualties of this new spirituality. Playing hooky from church has become a new national pastime.

A study of church behavior reveals that a large segment of the public is the actively churched. These are people who attend church once a month or more often. They constitute 45 percent of the adult population—the first time since public opinion surveys have been available that regular attenders represent a minority of adults. They are joined by the minimally churched (i.e., people whose attendance is generally infrequent and often unpredictable, accumulating to several times a year), who make up 8 percent of adults. One-third of the public (34 percent) fits the category of de-churched, those who were formerly regulars but have since dropped out. They are the fastest-growing segment. The other rapidly expanding group is the purely unchurched, a collection of individuals who have never attended a Christian church service. They are just 12 percent today but growing quickly due to the emergence of Millennials who have had and want no church experience. The last two segments together—46 percent of US adults—represent the unchurched.[1]

The data show that the number of unchurched adults in the United States has increased by nearly 60 percent in the past decade. Through the end of 2015, the estimated number of unchurched adults stood at 112 million. Combine that with the unchurched children and teenagers across the country, and the total swells to 151 million churchless people. In fact, during the past decade, the ranks of the churchless have grown by an astonishing thirty-eight million individuals. Although a handful of subgroups, such as evangelicals, have resisted the national impulse to abandon local churches, the vast majority of demographic subgroups are guilty of declining church attendance.

A pattern emerges among churchless people. In their younger years, an unchurched person's primary reason for distancing themselves from a church is their perception of the experience. Our research found that the churchless tend to consider Christians to be spiritually shallow; churches to be restrictive and overprotective, antagonistic to science, simplistic or judgmental in their approach to sexuality, and unfriendly to those who doubt. They also find the exclusivity of Christianity to be a turnoff. The older a person becomes, the more their objections revolve around the notion that church life simply does not provide sufficient value to justify their participation. About half of unchurched adults give some variation of this concern as their primary obstacle to church participation.[2]

In the past, men comprised a substantial majority of the unchurched. As women have lessened their devotion to church life, the gender balance is pretty even at this point. In fact, the demographic profile of churchless people looks quite similar to that of the overall population. Being unchurched is becoming normative.

Some of those without a church to call home will make their way back, but such a transition is becoming less and less likely as our society loses its confidence in and connection with churches. Consider this: even though most of the unchurched describe themselves as Christian (62 percent) and say they are spiritual people (65 percent), just half as many (30 percent) believe it is desirable to be known as a Christian and the same limited number possess a "very favorable" impression of Christianity. In total, three out of four churchless people are disinterested in corporate expressions of faith. These are independent, self-reliant individuals who distrust organizations and believe more in themselves than anything else.

Barely one-third of unchurched adults (36 percent) have what they consider to be an active relationship with God that influences their life today. Just one out of four believe the Bible would be an invaluable source of information to address difficult or challenging questions about matters of faith. Churchless people are more likely to cite problems with churches than to identify ways in which Christian congregations have added value to society.

Despite the barriers to engagement, two-thirds of the churchless noted that they have tried various ways of deepening their faith during the past month. Yet, despite such attempts at isolated spiritual development, six out of ten of them admit they are no more spiritually mature or advanced today than they were as a child! That truly underscores their distaste for church life: wanting to grow spiritually, making the effort, seeing little to no results from their efforts but continuing to resist the option of participating in church activities. Even the minority who said they might conceivably consider a church in the future cautioned that they would implement the one-strike rule: they might explore a single church and then give up the hunt if it does not work out.

Key Facts

- 46 percent of adults are unchurched—an increase from the 35 percent in 2005.
- The total number of unchurched Americans (including children and teenagers) rose from 112 million in 2005 to 151 million in 2015.
- 62 percent of the unchurched consider themselves to be Christian.
- 65 percent of the unchurched define themselves as "spiritual" people.
- 21 percent of the unchurched are born-again Christians (based on their theology, not self-description).
- 34 percent of the unchurched describe themselves as "deeply spiritual."
- 41 percent of the unchurched "strongly agree" that their religious faith is very important in their life today.
- 51 percent of the unchurched claim to be actively seeking something better spiritually than they have experienced.
- 59 percent of Americans disconnect from church life either permanently or for a prolonged period of time between the ages of fifteen and twenty-nine.

- 30 percent of the unchurched believe it is desirable to be known as a Christian in American society.

- 48 percent of the unchurched indicate they are not connected to a church because it provides no value (i.e., 15 percent say they have no interest, 13 percent have no reason to attend, 11 percent are too busy, 6 percent believe they can do religion at home, and 3 percent have not found a church they like).

- 14 percent of unchurched people said they are open to trying a new church.

Percentage of Adults Who Are Unchurched

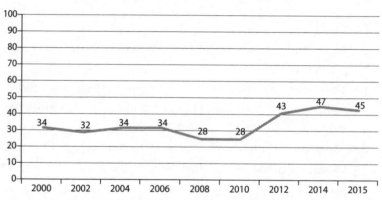

Sources: OmniPoll™ surveys conducted by Barna Group in January of each year shown. Sample sizes ranged from 1,000 to 1,028 each year from 2000–2012; 2,036 in 2014; and 2,005 in 2015.

Outlook and Interpretation

What is the compelling reason for unchurched people to engage with a church? From their perspective, they have been there, done that, glad to be gone. In general, they have no perceived need or interest in engaging. As they look at the value proposition offered by churches, it fails to meet their standards. They demand to know what the church has that they need badly enough to change their existing lifestyle and how the experience will be better this time around than when they left the church (as most unchurched people have) in the past.

Attracting churchless people to corporate faith usually requires more than a few incremental refinements in outreach strategy and tactics. This is about more than improved marketing and having greeters at the church's front door. Churches are facing a radically different outreach environment than existed a decade ago, including an antagonistic media that continually portrays churches in a negative light. The unchurched population is substantially larger and has a different demographic profile than in the past. To penetrate that population, churches must raise their game to meet more demanding and sophisticated expectations than ever. And, in most cases, the church community will have one shot at persuading the churchless to return for another experience.

Given the steady increase in the number of Millennials who become unchurched adults, the coming decade will be the first time in modern American history that the proportion of Americans who are churchless will exceed the 50 percent mark. That does not mean Christians will be unable to spiritually connect with the churchless, but it does suggest that inviting them to attend church services is not likely to be the primary way that meaningful spiritual connections are made. Research indicates that such connections are most likely to revolve around providing people with easily perceived value. Such value includes a sense of belonging, consistently facilitating a real experience with God, offering opportunities to impact the world, providing genuine life insight and wisdom, and giving families a chance to raise their children in a positive spiritual environment.[3] With increasing frequency, attending church services is an activity that occurs after believers have provided these examples of spiritual value to unchurched people in other environments and circumstances.

4
RELIGIOUS
EDUCATION

Summary

For many decades, the routine for most American households was the same: attend church services on Sunday morning, join a Sunday school class during an adjacent hour, and then return for a special service on Sunday night. Wednesday night featured the midweek service. That meant each committed Christian in America, adults as well as children, was exposed to an average of three or four religious teaching sessions each week, averaging roughly three hours of religious instruction every week. Beyond that, individuals often spent time reading the Bible and other religious books in an effort to discover more about their faith.

These certainly aren't the good old days of religious instruction by any stretch of the imagination. A slowly declining minority of adults attend Sunday worship services, where the average sermon length has dropped by more than 30 percent since 1980. Barely one out of ten adults attends a Sunday school class these days. Most churches have eliminated their Sunday or Wednesday evening services—and many have scratched both. In many churches, those events have been replaced by "small groups" that meet in people's homes, but attendance at those gatherings has also dropped from 23 percent to just 10 percent in the past decade. Further, Christians across the nation indicate that the emphasis in these meetings is more on developing a sense of community than providing insightful biblical instruction.[1]

Other sources of religious education have also fallen by the wayside. Christian publishing has shriveled to previously unthinkable dimensions, as the shrinking pool of Christian publishing houses prints fewer new Christian books each year for consumption by an audience that has been purchasing fewer spiritual books in recent years.[2] That coincides with a decline in personal Bible reading.

Oddly, these changes mean that perhaps the dominant source of Christian education is the media. Although Christian radio has experienced a transition of its own in recent years, from being primarily teaching-based to music-driven, there are still several hundred Christian teaching programs broadcast nationally via radio and television along with thousands of websites that provide substantive spiritual content from a biblical perspective. The typical American adult is now exposed to more Christian teaching through media sources than through live church experiences in any given week.[3]

One of the most intriguing reasons behind the transition from church-based to media-based Christian education has been the steadfast refusal of churches to address the issues that confound people in real life. A national study among conservative Christians who are spiritually active recently discovered that two-thirds of those believers (67 percent) unequivocally stated that they want their church to provide more teaching and information describing what the Bible teaches about current social and political issues.[4]

The study identified twenty-two current issues that a majority of conservative Christians described as being either "extremely" or "very important" for their church to address from the Scriptures. The issues of interest to conservative churchgoers were broad based, including controversial social issues (e.g., abortion and sexual identity), governance issues (government accountability, the appropriate role of government, rule of law), religious matters (religious persecution, America's Christian heritage, Islam), cultural concerns (cultural restoration, media, civil disobedience), and more.

This hunger for relevant teaching and biblical applications was equally common among men and women, although the research found that conservative churchgoers under the age of fifty were somewhat less interested in being exposed to such teaching on most of the topics examined. The topics for which younger adults were particularly less interested in learning what the Bible has to say were government authority, government accountability, patriotism, and Israel.[5]

Pastors' refusal to teach on the kinds of social and political issues examined, despite their congregants' undeniable interest, is a situation pastors grudgingly acknowledge. The study revealed that while more than 90 percent of theologically conservative pastors believe the Bible addresses all of these issues, very few pastors address those issues from the pulpit. For instance, while more than four out of five congregants wanted to hear teaching about the role of Israel, only one in three pastors claimed to have taught on that subject in recent years—and just one in four congregants could recall their pastor actually teaching on the topic. The proportion of churches that had addressed other critical issues was even lower: 13 percent of pastors claimed to have discussed gun rights, 12 percent said they spoke about educational reform, 10 percent dealt with individual privacy, 9 percent provided biblical perspectives on taxes and financial reform, and only 8 percent took on immigration.[6]

One consequence of the mismatch between content need and content delivery has been that millions of churchgoing adults have come to think of church attendance as an obligation rather than a value-added experience, largely because the focal point of the services is teaching on topics they consider well-intentioned but personally irrelevant or impractical. Just as significant, research reveals that millions of those who avoid church services (i.e., the unchurched)

do so expressly because they perceive church teaching to be discon-
nected from daily life.[7]

This deficit in Christian education is causing Christians to with-
draw from the cultural discussion regarding how to think about these
issues. One example of that isolation is the decline in interpersonal
evangelism. An equally startling example is the recent finding that
biblical Christians are less likely than other people to raise or debate
current social issues with friends who hold different worldviews because they feel ill-equipped to engage in such conversations.[8]

Key Facts

- Adult attendance in Sunday school classes has gone from 16
  percent in 1995 to 20 percent in 2005 to 12 percent in 2015.[9]
- Among born-again adults, attendance in Sunday school classes
  has seesawed from 33 percent in 1995 to 36 percent in 2005 to
  25 percent in 2015.[10]
- Participation in small groups that meet regularly for religious
  purposes, such as Bible study, prayer, or Christian fellowship,
  has changed from 17 percent in 1995 to 23 percent in 2005 to
  10 percent in 2015.[11]
- Among born-again adults, participation in small groups that
  meet regularly for religious purposes has gone from 34 percent
  in 1995 to 36 percent in 2005 to 26 percent in 2015.[12]
- In the last twenty years, church service attendance has declined
  by 21 percent. During that same period, small group participation has dropped 28 percent and Sunday school participation
  has declined by 29 percent.[13]
- A full two-thirds of conservative Christians—67 percent—said
  they want their church to provide them with more teaching about
  politically and culturally relevant topics, such as immigration,
  sexual identity, religious persecution, and civil disobedience.[14]

Religious Education Participation in a Typical Week

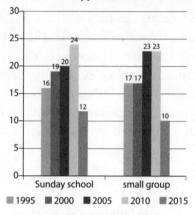

Sources: OmniPoll™ surveys conducted by Barna Group in January of each year shown. Sample sizes were 1,006 in 1995; 1,002 in 2000; 1,003 in 2005; 1,005 in 2010; and 2,005 in 2015.

Outlook and Interpretation

The implications of this trend are frightening for the Church. Biblical illiteracy is already high. The reduction in the amount of instruction adults—much less their children—are receiving is bound to leave us even more ill-informed about the substance of the Bible.

Churches, of course, could begin to turn that situation around by strategically increasing people's exposure to biblical teaching. However, the trend in church life is to reduce rather than increase church programming and to expedite rather than prolong people's time spent engaging in church events.

What would cause the current situation to change for the better? It would probably take a combination of factors, such as seminaries producing pastors who have both the courage and biblical training to teach on the issues of the day; congregations evaluating pastors on the basis of the quality, breadth, biblical substance, and applicability of the teaching rather than the multifaceted comfort it provides; pastors reconceptualizing the purpose of their teaching; denominations supporting their pastors who address current social and political issues from a biblical vantage point; and issue-focused parachurch ministries providing preaching-ready notes for pastors to draw from as they become more deeply acquainted with the issues and related biblical content.

During America's colonial years, pastors consistently spoke about the issues of the day and challenged their people to study, understand, and discuss these matters. A voting population that lacks comprehension of the issues and their biblical connotations is vulnerable. If pastors step up to provide compelling teaching about the various facets of contemporary life, our culture has a greater hope of being restored to virtue.

The ultimate end of a heightened investment in practical biblical instruction must be clearly understood. It would be the widespread embrace of a biblical worldview, wherein Christians possess sufficient scriptural knowledge and comprehension to make intelligent and biblically sound choices. With less than 10 percent of the adult born-again population currently possessing a biblical worldview, there is plenty of room for growth![15]

5
THE
BIBLE

Summary

Americans do not buy books as often as they used to. But more than nine out of ten households in the country contain a Bible. In fact, the typical home has four or five sitting around somewhere.[1]

Most Americans have a positive impression of the Bible. Despite radical shifts in spiritual perspectives, most people still consider it to be "holy literature." In fact, it is the only book that at least one out of every ten Americans thinks of as holy (and eight out of every ten consider it to be such). The Bible also outshines every other book ever written as the one that most Americans would say has had the greatest impact on humanity. No other book comes close: people select the Bible as the most influential book by a twelve-to-one margin over its closest rival, which happens to be the Koran.[2]

However, Americans are not quite sure about the veracity of Scripture, despite its lofty perch as the most influential book. Only about one-third contend that it is totally accurate in all of the principles it teaches. That is a significant decline from fifteen years ago when one-half of the public considered the Bible to be totally accurate in the principles it communicates.[3] While a large majority considers it to be inspired by God Himself, almost half argue that it contains errors.[4]

Perhaps the seeming inconsistencies have more to do with people's biblical ignorance than with God's composition. A minority—just one out of every five adults—has read the Bible from cover to cover.[5] Even though a relative handful (8 percent) believes one must have professional training to correctly interpret the biblical narrative, the Bible benefits those who consistently read it.[6] However, only about one-third of adults read from the Bible during a typical week—a substantial decline from past decades, when a majority of people sought guidance from the Scriptures on a regular, if not daily, basis. The percentage of adults who read the Bible during the week, other than when they are at a church event, has plummeted by fourteen percentage points in just the past five years![7]

Because of the halfhearted attention Americans give to God's Word these days, research shows that people's knowledge of its content is slipping. They generally grasp a few of the major concepts pretty well. Nearly three-quarters believe that the Bible's main message is either God is love or He wants a relationship with the people He has created. Perhaps thanks to Christmas songs and other seasonal expressions, a similar proportion of people know Jesus Christ was born in Bethlehem. Perhaps surprisingly, almost six out of ten adults know Isaac was the son of Abraham, and a small majority even knows that the apostle Paul was also known as Saul.[8]

Things go downhill from there though. Not quite half of the public can identify the names of the first four books of the New Testament, known as the Gospels. A large share believes that John the Baptist was one of Jesus's apostles. Almost half contend that one of the Bible's teachings is that God helps those who help themselves. (In fact, it teaches quite the opposite: human beings are incapable of helping themselves, thus necessitating the sacrificial death and resurrection of Jesus Christ on our behalf, the subsequent indwelling of the Holy Spirit to provide guidance, and the tangible direction found in the

Bible itself.) Only a minority are able to name the first five books of the Bible. Three-quarters of all adults incorrectly believe the Bible is available in all of the world's languages. Millions of Americans believe that Joan of Arc was Noah's wife (one out of twelve people goofed up on this) and one out of seven believes Sodom and Gomorrah were married. These kinds of statistics rightfully send chills down the spines of pastors.[9]

To their credit, most people do not consider themselves to be either "extremely" or "moderately" knowledgeable about the Bible. But it is odd that a book that is so widely owned and seemingly appreciated, if not revered, gets so little attention from people.[10]

Maybe that disconnect between the Bible's image and how much energy people put into knowing its contents is because they're not really convinced it can make a difference in their lives. Studies show that less than half of the public believes the Bible contains everything a person needs to know to live a meaningful life.[11] People may also be struggling to accept the idea that the Bible is much different from any other respected religious literature. For instance, less than one-third of adults firmly believe the Bible is substantively different from the spiritual truths conveyed in other widely read religious literature such as the Koran and the Book of Mormon.[12] And when it comes right down to it, there is no particular aspect of life related to which a majority of Americans want guidance from the Bible. The most common life challenges for which people wish they had biblical insight include dealing with serious illnesses or death, family conflict, and parenting. However, fewer than three out of ten adults registered interest in receiving scriptural insights related to each of those areas.[13]

Nevertheless, a bare majority say they would like to see the Bible have greater influence on American society. (That majority is somewhat mitigated by the one-fifth who would like to see it have less authority.)[14] And while some people are not keen on the exact words of the Bible, a majority seems interested in advancing its principles. For example, two-thirds of adults argue that it is important for the public schools to teach the Bible's core values to school children.[15] A growing number of Christian leaders have been expressing their concern that biblical allusions in public speech are being curtailed by the politically correct police, but three-quarters of Americans do not presently experience or fear such intolerance.[16] Then again, that may be because so few of them discuss or share biblical content in their conversations.

Key Facts

- Overall, 91 percent of US households own at least one Bible.
- In 2015, 33 percent read from the Bible, other than while they were at a church event, during the past week. In 2010, 47 percent had done so. The proportion of born-again adults reading the Bible during the week dropped during that same time period from 68 percent to 59 percent.[17]
- About one-third contend that the Bible is totally accurate in all of the principles it teaches.[18]
- Only 20 percent of all adults have read the Bible from cover to cover. Among born-again Christians, nearly twice as many (36 percent), but still a minority, have done so. Evangelicals are the only population segment among which a majority (60 percent) has read the Bible from cover to cover.[19]
- 45 percent of adults say they are "extremely" or "moderately" knowledgeable about the Bible. Among born-again Christians, a slightly higher proportion (55 percent) makes that claim.[20]
- 49 percent of adults strongly believe the Bible contains everything a person needs to know to live a meaningful life. A much larger percentage of the born-again population (79 percent) has adopted that point of view.[21]
- Barely half of the adult population (51 percent) wants the Bible to have greater influence on American society, while 19 percent would like it to have less authority.[22]

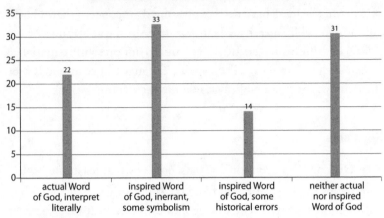

What Americans Believe about the Bible

Source: Barna Group, OmniPoll™1-15PH, N=1,016, January 2015.

Outlook and Interpretation

The Bible is fighting an uphill battle for acceptance and perceived value in America. Evidence shows that more and more people—especially those under the age of thirty—are losing interest in the Bible, partly because they have little trust in its accuracy and applicability to today's fast-moving, sophisticated world. To a growing number of people—especially those who describe themselves as "spiritual but not religious"—the Bible is just one of several options for religious guidance.

At the same time, enough older Americans have had years of exposure to biblical content so that a solid majority still appreciate the importance of the Bible, both historically and even for our present society. Despite the uproar raised by mainstream media about the illegitimate use of the Bible in public policy, public education, business, and other public spaces, most citizens still want the Bible to have a presence and influence in churches, schools, government, and their own homes. Whether they are courageous enough to let that view be heard and to support that perspective is another matter.

That fewer and fewer Americans possess a worldview predominantly shaped by the Bible is a testament to the "relevant" preaching offered in growing numbers of churches, as well as to the absence of biblical teaching and discussion in homes and schools. Because our studies have convincingly shown that a person's Bible knowledge is largely developed during their formative years, the absence of Bible training during the childhood and adolescent years of most young Americans argues against the likelihood of the United States becoming a biblically literate country in the foreseeable future. The Bible's role in our society will continue to diminish without an intentional and concerted effort on the part of those who appreciate it.

6 EVANGELICALS

Summary

Few population segments generate as much heat or garner as much attention as evangelicals. Although they comprise only 7 percent of the adult public, they have disproportionate influence in our culture. Their influence is driven by their strong conviction that the purpose of their life is to love God by serving and obeying Him, and that their Christian faith is meant to be lived wholeheartedly, not merely believed intellectually.[1]

Evangelicals are an example of a niche that is small but mighty. Even within church circles they are dwarfed by non-evangelical born-again Christians (who are about 30 percent of the population) and notional Christians (people who consider themselves to be Christian but have not confessed their sins and asked Christ to save them, a segment that constitutes about 40 percent of the population). In other words, among all of the adults who consider themselves to be Christian, evangelicals are outnumbered ten to one by those who do not embrace biblical positions on sin, salvation, and Scripture.

While my research has shown that born-again Christians, on the whole, are barely distinguishable from others in society, evangelicals are consistently distinct from all other segments of adults who consider themselves to be Christian—and radically different from those who do not claim to be Christian. When compared to the five macro-faith subgroups in the United States—evangelicals, non-evangelical born agains, notional Christians, non-Christian faiths, atheists/agnostics—evangelical Christians are the only segment in which a majority have read the entire Bible; read the Bible every day; regularly listen to Christian-music radio; regularly read Christian nonfiction; attend church services every week; and will attend church, read the Bible, and pray during a typical week.[2]

The distinctives of evangelicals do not end there. They are the only subgroup of the five in which a majority believe Satan is a living entity; believe that being a good person is not enough to earn a place in Heaven; firmly believe they have a personal commitment to spread the gospel; recognize a difference in the principles taught by the Bible, Koran, and Book of Mormon; and say they are very committed to having a deeper spiritual experience than they have had in the past.[3]

Evangelicals are also the only one of the five subgroups in which a majority describe themselves as politically conservative and most say their faith influences their political views a great deal. A majority of evangelicals are registered Republicans—the only faith subgroup for which that is true.[4]

The differences go on. Compared to the other faith subgroups, they are the most likely to be concerned about America's moral condition and the least likely to characterize homosexuality, cohabitation, abortion, drunkenness, gambling, divorce, adultery, pornography, and suicide as morally acceptable behaviors. They are the most likely to donate time and money to churches, to share their faith with non-Christians, and to believe the Bible is inerrant. They are unabashedly pro-life, opposed to same-sex marriage, want the Bible and prayer back in schools, and argue that the Bible does not have enough influence in American society.[5]

And so on—you get the drift. Whereas born-again Christians who are not evangelical generally reflect the lifestyles, attitudes, and tastes of the nation as a whole, evangelicals invariably stand out from every other faith segment—including those who regularly show up at church services and events. While evangelicals are not a perfect representation of biblical standards, they are so much closer to reflecting biblical ways that they seem to have little in common with the rest of the culture.

And that culture never fails to bring these differences to the attention of evangelicals.

In the same way that a miniscule but determined proportion of the public—the 3 percent who constitute the gay population—diligently pursued national acceptance of same-sex marriage and other gay rights, so have evangelicals been the tiny but dominant segment defending and promoting a conservative interpretation of biblical values. Even though non-evangelical born-again Christians share many theological perspectives and experiences with evangelicals, they are not nearly as devoted to integrating their faith into every dimension of life or applying biblical principles within the social and political arena.

In fact, while evangelicals are a solid, unified voting block—there is generally greater than 80 percent consistency in the social and political views of evangelicals, and their recent voting choices reflect similar unity—the born-again Christians who are *not* evangelical are divided and inconsistent in their views on matters of public policy, political party identification, morality, and candidate preference. The sheer size of the born-again constituency should make them a cherished and respected segment, and their shared spiritual foundation should make them a unified force. Sadly, they are simply an unreliable, up-for-grabs accumulation of ideologically and theologically confused people.[6]

Surprisingly, the percentage of adults who are evangelicals has not changed in the thirty years it has been measured by the Barna Group. During that same period, the proportion of what are widely called the "nones"—those who do not believe in God, who don't know if they believe in God, or who don't care one way or the other—has quadrupled to become approximately double the size of the evangelical body (14 percent) and is the fastest-growing faith segment in America.[7]

One of the most noteworthy attributes of evangelicals is their steadiness over time. Whereas most Americans who identify them-selves as Christians have changed some of their core religious beliefs and behaviors over time, evangelicals are perhaps the single most predictable and reliable segment of the population. You may not like what they believe or how they put those beliefs into practice, but you will always be able to tell where they stand and why—last year, this year, next year, and next decade.

Key Facts

Religious behavior during a typical week:

Behavior	Evangelical		Non-evang'l Born Again		Notional		Non-Christian		Atheist/Agnostic	
	2015	2005	2015	2005	2015	2005	2015	2005	2015	2005
Pray to God	100%	99%	97%	95%	81%	79%	75%	65%	29%	16%
Read the Bible	88	86	63	52	28	22	42	19	17	4
Attend religious services	84	84	61	49	39	30	27	19	7	5
Attend small group	61	40	30	16	15	4	23	9	4	2
Attend Sunday school	53	42	32	19	12	5	13	11	0	4

Sources: Barna Group, OmniPoll™1-15C, N=1,821 adults, January 2015; Barna Group, OmniPoll™1-05, N=1,003 adults, January 2005.

Views on morally acceptable behavior:

Behavior	Evangelical	Non-evang'l Born Again	Notional	Non-Christian	Atheist/Agnostic
Sexual relationship with opposite sex, not married	1%	33%	56%	62%	87%
Cohabitation	2	41	68	76	95
Viewing pornography	0	23	46	54	79
Using profanity	5	25	49	41	78
Having an abortion	1	17	40	68	80

Source: Barna Group, OmniPoll™ 1-14C, N=2,036 adults, February 2014.

Religious beliefs:

Behavior	Evangelical	Non-evang'l Born Again	Notional	Non-Christian	Atheist/ Agnostic
Bible is true, has no errors	99%	84%	44%	27%	8%
Jesus lived a sinless life	100	55	27	31	20
Bible contains everything you need to live meaningful life	98	74	41	15	4
Koran, Book of Mormon, and Bible teach different truths	87	35	19	21	19
Your faith influences your political views a great deal	82	40	24	40	7
Very committed to having a deeper spiritual experience than have ever had before	80	35	8	23	2
Bible and politics don't mix	26	42	56	74	87

Sources: Barna Group, OmniPoll™1-15C, N=2,002 adults, January 2015; and Barna Group, OmniPoll™1-13OL, N=1,078 adults, January 2013.

Outlook and Interpretation

Evangelicals have long served as a boogeyman for the mainstream media and liberal politicians. The data suggest that if evangelicals loosen their grip on biblical principles and consequently ignore the nation's decline in Judeo-Christian morality, abandon traditional values, and fail to energetically defend conservative governance based on biblical ideals, then essentially no one will be consistently blocking the path to a fairly rapid and dramatic leftward move by American culture. An existing danger sign related to that scenario is how few evangelicals currently engage their liberal friends and co-workers in conversation about the important issues of the day; less than one-third currently have such dialogue.[8]

Many conservative analysts posit that if such a swing happens, the intense desire of leading liberals to reconstruct the moral and philosophical foundations of the nation will permanently alter the nature, health, and trajectory of the republic. Evangelicals have become, by default, the conservative, biblical moral conscience of an

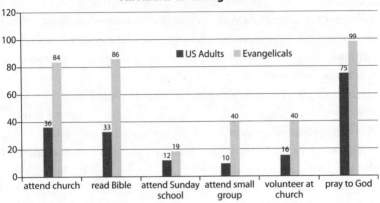

Religious Behavior in a Typical Week, All Adults vs. Evangelicals

Source: Barna Group, OmniPoll™ 1-15C, N=2,005, January 2015.

increasingly immoral nation. They cannot afford to falter in that role if the United States is to retain its Christian heritage or honor God's ways. If evangelicals do, indeed, grow weary in the battle to uphold biblical principles, then the battle will be lost for the foreseeable future.

For the rest of this decade, evangelicals will experience an intense public relations campaign against their character, motivations, and objectives. Given America's politically correct environment, you can count on evangelicals being portrayed as hate-mongering, narrow-minded, old-fashioned, bigoted religious zealots. For that characterization to change, both Gen Xers and Millennials would have to alter their current perceptions and concerns about evangelicals—a shift that is highly unlikely.

And for the evangelical population to grow, converts would have to be drawn from those two antagonistic generations. To better understand how unlikely this is to happen, realize that research shows that a declining proportion of Protestant churches are teaching the "hard truths" from the Scriptures—truths that correspond to the worldview held by evangelicals. With so much momentum moving against them, including the aging of the group, it is very plausible that the proportion of evangelicals will decline from its already-minimal level of 7 percent. Granted, church history provides examples of biblical communities that resisted the attacks of secularism and even used those attacks to stimulate an evangelical resurgence. One lesson from those examples, though, is the importance of great leadership.[9] Does the American evangelical community today have visionary, skillful, devoted leaders who are ready to embrace such a challenge?

While evangelical shrinkage is not likely to reduce the passion that the remaining evangelicals have for promoting a biblical worldview and the lifestyle that accompanies it—and to salvage American society in the process—one cannot fault those who question the ability of evangelicals to redirect America back to the heart of God. It is a righteous cause and a noble battle to wage but definitely a steep, uphill journey.

7
LIFE
TRANSFORMATION

Summary

The Christian Church is faced with a major paradox. On the one hand, its leaders contend they are doing a good job of discipling people—that is, helping those who claim to be Christians to follow Christ. Surveys among pastors reveal them to be quite pleased with the spiritual condition of their congregants and planning to continue on the same course of action to keep producing the same outcomes they have been generating.[1]

On the other hand, the Christian Church is rapidly losing influence in American society. Some argue that it has little to no influence. Indeed, the research consistently reveals little discernible difference in the core behaviors and lifestyle attitudes and values of born-again Christians when compared with other Americans. Regarding indicators of religious behavior, the differences are noteworthy: born-again adults are more likely than others to attend church services, read the Bible, pray, donate money to churches and nonprofit organizations, attend Christian education classes, and participate in small groups that meet for religious purposes. On indicators of lifestyle behaviors, covering activities from divorce, debt, and gambling to life priorities and the use of profanity, the differences between born-again adults and others are small to nonexistent.

When all the smoke and mirrors are removed from the discussion, most churchgoing people in America have no idea what the objectives of their religious pursuits are other than to be a better person, to believe in the existence and goodness of Jesus Christ, to keep God happy, and to be a good church member. When pushed to describe in practical terms what these things mean and how they can best accomplish these objectives, alarmingly few people possess viable answers and almost nobody has a plan. They assume that attending church regularly, praying and reading the Bible occasionally, and completing a church program or two designed to facilitate "spiritual maturity" will do the job.

Churches and their leaders facilitate this belief by aggressively promoting participation in a variety of programs and pointing to participation rates as an indicator of people's spiritual health. In turn, that approach is largely dictated by the way in which churches gauge ministry success, which is accomplished by measuring attendance, donations, program involvement, staff expansion, and space requirements. The assumption is that an increase in bodies, programs, dollars, employees, and square footage reflects a dynamic, healthy, growing ministry through which lives are being changed. Unfortunately, research within and across churches demonstrates that these assumptions are faulty: virtually no correlation exists between those factors and life transformation.

In fact, a massive research project that traced the spiritual development of Americans who identify as Christians revealed that genuine spiritual transformation is shockingly rare. To become Christlike, people must experience ten stops on the journey to wholeness. During the first three stops, people progress from being unaware of the concept of sin, to feeling indifferent toward the concept, to showing concern about the personal implications of sin but without taking any related action. Almost two-thirds of Americans never get beyond stop 3 on the journey, even though tens of millions of them regularly attend Christian churches.

Those who master stop 4 of the journey acknowledge that they are sinners, ask for God's forgiveness for their sins, and embrace Jesus Christ as their Savior. They quickly move to stop 5 of the journey, where they become immersed in religious activity with the hope of becoming more Christlike, or at least a better person. About one-quarter of the nation's population gets to and remains at one of these two stops.

Stop 6 of the journey is a place of spiritual discontent. While about one out of every ten adults reaches this place of spiritual reconsideration and recalibration, half are so overwhelmed by its requirements that they wind up dropping out of spiritual pursuit altogether while the other half continue forward.

The last four stops on the journey are the most challenging—and indisputably the least widely pursued and most rewarding. Stop 7 is where the individual experiences brokenness of sin, self, and societal control. It is the place where one makes the choice to truly pursue godliness rather than worldliness. Once that choice has been made, the individual can experience total submission and surrender to God's will and His ways (stop 8), followed by a life characterized by fully loving God (stop 9) and then people (stop 10) in Christlike ways. People produce different types of fruit at each stop along the way, but those who reach the final three ports of the journey stand out as highly unusual and laudable human beings. They are notable because of who they have become rather than what they have done or what they know. Ultimately, that is what holistic spiritual transformation is about: who you have become rather than what you have accomplished or what you have learned.

Unfortunately, seminaries do not teach pastors to encourage and facilitate such transformation; elder boards do not evaluate pastors based on their ability to foster transformation; sermons rarely address the practical realities of transformation; our culture, supported by churches, successfully implores adults to reject or avoid brokenness; and people doggedly pursue success and comfort rather than holiness. Consequently, most church-going people are involved in religion rather than genuine discipleship.

Jesus taught His followers that transformation is measured by the fruit we produce. He could not have been more transparent than when He told His disciples, "When you produce much fruit, you are my true disciples" (John 15:8). He also informed them that the most desirable fruit is when we love God and other people with all of our hearts, souls, minds, and strength (see Mark 12:30–31). Those are the final stops on the transformational journey, reflecting the ultimate fruit of how Christ has changed us.

In light of those exhortations, it is discouraging to find that in America, eight out of ten adults claim to be Christian, about half that many attend Christian church services at least once a month, only one out of three has confessed their sinfulness and asked Jesus to be their Savior, and just one out of every one hundred has been spiritually broken, has surrendered and submitted themselves to God, and is engaged in loving Him and His creation as their ultimate life pursuit.

It seems likely that this reality, more than any other explanation, is why the Church in America lacks influence on the world. It is not for lack of enough churches or the absence of appealing programs or funding. Genuine and consistent love is what will change the world, but the research indicates that not enough Christ followers embody and express the love of God to impress a society that is desperately searching for such love.

Key Facts

- Few Americans get past the halfway mark of the transformational journey. Currently, 64 percent are on stop 1, 2, or 3 of the ten-stop spiritual journey—what believers might consider to be the "pre-salvation stops." Another 25 percent are on stop 4 or 5, having confessed their sins, accepted Christ as their Savior, and become more deeply involved in religious activities. About 6 percent are parked at stop 6, born again but wrestling with spiritual discontent. The remaining 5 percent are all born again and distributed among the last four stops: spiritual brokenness, surrender and submission, complete intimacy with and love of God, and consistent and encompassing love of people.[2]

- 11 percent of all adults have a conversation about faith in a typical week with someone who believes differently than they do.[3]
- 16 percent believe absolute moral truth exists and is defined in the Bible.[4]
- 18 percent claim they are totally committed to investing themselves in spiritual development.[5]
- 20 percent say the most important decisions they have ever made were asking God for forgiveness and inviting Jesus to be their Lord and Savior.[6]
- 21 percent say it is imperative for a person to be connected to a community of faith if they want to mature spiritually.[7]
- 22 percent state they are completely dependent on God.[8]
- 19 percent say they are very committed to having deeper spiritual experiences than they have had in the past.[9]
- 20 percent firmly believe they have a clear sense of what God wants them to do with their life.[10]
- 34 percent say they know God is pleased with their priorities and life choices.[11]
- Among people who believe Jesus was a real person, 16 percent claim they make the "greatest possible effort" to follow His example; 10 percent claim they come "very close" to following His example.[12]

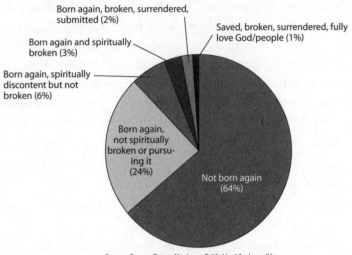

Where Americans Are on Their Spiritual Journey

Born again, broken, surrendered, submitted (2%)

Saved, broken, surrendered, fully love God/people (1%)

Born again and spiritually broken (3%)

Born again, spiritually discontent but not broken (6%)

Born again, not spiritually broken or pursuing it (24%)

Not born again (64%)

Source: George Barna, *Maximum Faith: Live Like Jesus,* (Ventura, CA: Metaformation, 2011). Updated with surveys by Barna Group, 2015.

Outlook and Interpretation

Churches across the country are undergoing dramatic changes. More megachurches dominate the landscape than ever before. A startling number of multicampus churches have also taken root. A new generation of pastors is assuming control of the nation's pastorates, replacing the Builders and Boomers who came before them. Billions of dollars are raised for church-based ministry. Midweek and Sunday evening programs have been curtailed by a rapidly growing number of congregations. Denominational divisions are being reconsidered in favor of unity across organizations. Women have been hired as pastors in a record-breaking number of churches. Multiethnic congregations have become a more common reality.

And yet, few people allow God to break them of sin, self, and societal control in favor of true, costly discipleship. The changes that have been championed in the church are shifts in form more than substance. The church is producing the same kinds of people; they are simply exposed to different formats and structures.

Until the church raises up preachers who are not afraid to speak the truth about the necessity and beauty of brokenness, even if it produces a decline in attendance, true spiritual renewal is unlikely. Until people recognize that transformation is a goal, not anathema, cheap grace will abound. Until the church recognizes that people grow most effectively when coached or mentored by one or two fellow sojourners who are one or two stops ahead of them on the journey, rather than by just listening to more teaching from highly educated expositors, people's spiritual development will be stunted. Until fruit is measured rather than attendance, program participation, giving, and organizational expansion, we, as the Church, cannot hope to grow a body of people who imitate Christ.

As the American Church experiences social persecution, perhaps those challenges will facilitate the kinds of changes that will create opportunities for real transformation. Persecution and hardship are the most reliable triggers for change. Hopefully people will not simply try to comfortably adapt to the new, harsher circumstances and compromise their biblical calling to be Christlike.

Or perhaps enough people will grow tired of "churchianity" and religion and devote themselves to completing the rich spiritual journey God has prepared for His people. During various times in human history—i.e., the great awakenings and revivals of the past—the Holy Spirit stirred people to become authentic followers of Christ. The cultural circumstances seem ripe for such a spiritual turnaround in America today.

PART 2

GOVERNMENT AND POLITICS

8

GOVERNMENT
SATISFACTION

Summary

During the past quarter century, Americans have become increasingly wary—and weary—of government. Their concerns and complaints are most profoundly related to the federal government, but people are suspicious about the motives and performance of state and local governments too. Once upon a time it was considered an honor to serve in the government, and elected officials were respected if not revered. These days political parties are having a tough time persuading qualified individuals to run for public office, and for good reason: the process itself is grueling and the reputation of those who run or get elected often takes a beating. Indeed, parents rarely encourage their children to set goals such as running for Congress or president anymore.

An overwhelming majority of Americans harbors negative views of the federal government in all its shapes and forms. These negative perceptions are pervasive, cutting across all of the usual dividing lines: political party affiliation, racial groups, age cohorts, gender, regions, and socioeconomic segments. It is ironic that deep-seated personal animosity toward the federal government is one of the few political matters that people of all types agree on.

The depth of public dissatisfaction with the federal government is breathtaking. Large majorities are dissatisfied with its performance[1] and are unhappy with the direction in which it is moving the country.[2] The government has also instilled declining confidence among the public[3] and leaves most people either frustrated (62 percent) or angry (19 percent) with its efforts.[4] Only a handful of people (6 percent) feel sure that the federal government has the public's best interests at heart. In fact, most (85 percent) would go so far as to argue that most elected officials are more interested in protecting the needs of special interest groups than those of the people who elected them to office.[5]

Gallup's probing about the nation's top problems consistently determines that the federal government's poor performance has risen to the top of that list.[6] In fact, most adults believe the signers of the Declaration of Independence would be disappointed by the nature of governance in America these days.[7] Matters have gotten so bad that almost half of the public says the federal government's power and behavior pose an immediate threat to the rights and freedoms of American citizens.[8]

One particular survey conducted by a notoriously pro-Democratic Party polling firm, which is hard to take seriously, reported that the public has a higher opinion of cockroaches, used car salesmen, root canals, lice, and colonoscopies than it has of Congress. In defense of our elected legislators, the report points out that Congress did manage to outpoll telemarketers, Ebola, gonorrhea, and playground bullies.[9]

Based on the results from a plethora of *reliable* national surveys, however, it is clear that a substantial majority of people are displeased with the federal government, and that majority is steadily growing.

But empty feelings aren't driving Americans' distaste for the country's largest level of government. The national distress stems from the perception of mediocre performance. Adults believe that, on average, the federal government wastes about fifty-one cents of every dollar it spends.[10] Most people argue that the government tries to do too much, its efforts to regulate business do more harm than good, and it governs ineffectively and inefficiently.[11] Since 2010, more than six out of every ten adults have been dissatisfied with the way the nation is being governed.[12]

The individuals involved in the process of governing are chastised as well. Most Americans say top government officials are guilty of unethical behavior.[13] Most public officials disappoint the people who voted for them.[14] Voters contend that most elected leaders cannot be trusted to do what's right.[15] And the performance and approval ratings of all of the top federal leaders—from the president, House, and Senate to federal agencies—are consistently below 50 percent approval. Many of our federal agencies receive approval ratings below 20 percent.[16]

Americans feel increasingly hopeless about the state of the nation and its future. The federal government, with more than 4 million employees across the land, is our nation's biggest employer—bigger than Wal-Mart, McDonald's, and Target, who combined have a million fewer employees than the Washington bureaucracy.[17] That massive government regulates (and taxes) just about everything that breathes or moves. Many people contend it has taken on the aura of an unstoppable, out-of-control ogre. Numerous polls display nuances of the public regarding the federal government, including the common belief that it is incapable of solving the nation's problems, it will never change for the better, and that a single public official cannot make a positive difference (so, by inference, why bother to vote or get involved).[18]

That dark mood has produced a nation that is cynical about its own government, increasingly pessimistic about its future, feeling personally powerless, and open to a degree of isolationism that has not existed for a long time. People are increasingly selfish because they feel they have no choice: they believe their government is not looking out for them, so they need to grab for everything they can get before society takes advantage of them.

Key Facts

Amount of confidence people have in government:

	Great Deal		Great Deal/ Fair Amount	
	2014	2004	2014	2004
Legislative branch	3%	7%	28%	60%
Executive branch	14	31	43	58
Judicial branch	10	14	61	65
Agencies/departments of federal government	10	42	n/a	n/a
Your state government	19	16	62	67
Your local government	24	21	72	68

Source: Gallup Organization, http://www.gallup.com/poll/5392/trust-government.aspx.

- Americans estimate that the amount of each tax dollar wasted by the government varies by level of government: federal waste estimated to be fifty-one cents per dollar; state government waste estimated to be forty-two cents per dollar; local government waste believed to be thirty-seven cents per dollar.[19]

- 56 percent say government is almost always wasteful and inefficient.[20]

- Three-quarters of adults (78 percent) believe most elected officials don't care what people like them think.[21]

- Almost three-fourths of the public (71 percent) realize the nation is greatly divided when it comes to the most important values.[22]

- Feelings toward the federal government vary: 17 percent say they are content with it, 66 percent are frustrated, 19 percent are angry.[23]

- Just 3 percent say they can always trust the government in Washington to do what is right, with another 21 percent saying they can trust them to do so most of the time.[24]
- Two-thirds (66 percent) worry about how much information the government has about them.[25]
- Only 6 percent say they are very sure the government has their best interests in mind; 7 percent say Congress does; 15 percent claim the president does.[26]
- Two-thirds argue that the government will never change for the better.[27]

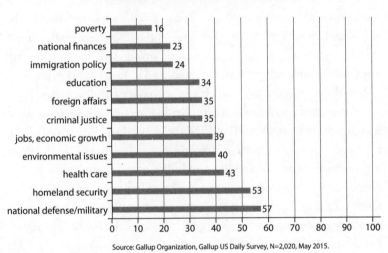

**Satisfaction with Aspects
of Federal Government Performance**

Source: Gallup Organization, Gallup US Daily Survey, N=2,020, May 2015.

Outlook and Interpretation

In some ways, the anger directed toward politicians and public officials is unfair: public officials alone did not create the fundamental shift in values that has led to the country's present dilemma. Parents, pastors, and educators are at least as much at fault—probably much more so—as we consider who has been responsible for allowing children and young adults to ignore biblical principles in favor of a secular worldview, embrace a new set of moral standards, pursue postmodern lifestyles, and adopt a version of American history and citizenship that diminishes the significance of family, faith, freedom, and truth. Political leaders take the fall for a job poorly done by those whose primary job it is to raise each new generation of Americans.

However, leadership is about promoting a shared vision that facilitates the common good. In American society, the common good has always been tied to biblical principles and godly outcomes—and, with some notable exceptions, that approach worked astoundingly well for more than two hundred years. Changing course without a consensual alternative vision to clearly guide us has resulted in the moral and social anarchy that befalls us today. Elected officials cannot duck responsibility for failing to provide strong, visionary leadership anchored by society's proven, accepted, and long-standing principles.

But the country is now stuck in the midst of political gridlock, animosity, and chaos, essentially divided between those who want less government intrusion and control, and those who are willing to accept more government dominion and less personal freedom as long as they are personally and holistically taken care of by the government. Can America return to a more limited government, with fewer public services, and retain the level of freedom that remains? It would be exceedingly difficult to get Uncle Sam, the nation's generous but demanding Sugar Daddy, to peacefully and gracefully reduce his stature. If it does happen, the transition will take years of reshaping the thinking, behavior, values, and expectations of Americans—especially those under the age of forty.

Unless some extraordinary leaders emerge who can guide the nation toward a less government-reliant path, the United States will most likely continue to pursue the European model of more government, less freedom, reduced personal opportunities, and diminished productivity. Even if such leadership arrives in time to stop the march toward greater government control, a long-term turnaround will not occur unless parents, educators, and clergy (among others) step up to alter the direction and training that future generations of American youth receive. A national transformation toward becoming a more independent, industrious, and freedom-appreciating populace is possible, but it will come neither easily nor quickly—and will require energy and commitment.

9
POLITICAL ENGAGEMENT

Summary

Civic participation comes in many forms. A review of eight of the most commonly measured forms indicates that all of them have been stable or in decline over the past decade.

The act of engagement that gets the most attention is voting. Overall, the Census Bureau estimates that about 65 percent of the voting-eligible population is registered to vote.[1] However, a large share of the people who are eligible to vote do not turn out to vote. During presidential elections, about 58 percent of citizens eighteen or older actually cast a ballot. In midterm elections—the two years before or after a presidential election when there is no presidential race but there are important statewide and local races, as well as initiatives and referenda to be decided by voters—slightly fewer than four out of ten adults participate. The 2014 election had a record-low turnout of 36.6 percent.[2]

As much as some bemoan the public's lack of voting in elections, a review of the historical trends shows that our current level of voting apathy has been in place since the turn of the century—the *twentieth* century. From the 1850s through 1900, roughly three-quarters of voting-age citizens voted in presidential elections. That dropped to two-thirds during the first decade of the 1900s and has been within a few percentage points of 60 percent turnout ever since. The average turnout for presidential elections in the first decade of our current century was 56.1 percent and slightly higher in 2012 (58.6 percent), thanks largely to the history-making presence of a black candidate and the use of the most sophisticated technology ever utilized to facilitate voter identification and turnout.

Similarly, midterm election turnout from 1850 through 1900 averaged 64 percent or more but has been in the 36 to 45 percent range since 1910. The combined average of 39.2 percent in 2010 and 2014 is the lowest decadal average since the 1910 decade and notably lower than the norm recorded in recent decades.[3]

The electorate for the 2014 midterm election was less than committed to carrying out its role in the electoral process with energy and excellence. Only one-third of the electorate (33 percent) had given "quite a lot" or "some" thought to the election; only one-third (32 percent) described themselves as "extremely motivated to vote"; and just 37 percent claimed to be "more enthusiastic than usual" about voting.[4] The result, as indicated, was a record-low turnout.

With media commentary about our political condition seemingly inescapable, you might be surprised to learn how few people engage in any given political activity. For instance, only one out of seven adults (15 percent) has donated any money to a political campaign or candidate in the past two years. One out of eight adults (12 percent) has attended a campaign event in the past two years. One out of every twelve adults (8 percent) has worked for or volunteered to help a campaign or candidate during that time. Even the two most common political activities, other than voting, have been undertaken by a minority of citizens. About four out of ten (42 percent) have discussed politics with someone during a typical week, and about one out of four (28 percent) has contacted a political official.[5]

However, measuring a fairly limited number of conventional political activities such as those identified above does not provide a comprehensive portrait of how active Americans are in the broader spectrum of political matters. Pew Research Center discovered that nearly three-quarters of US adults (72 percent) have been involved in one or more of a list of twenty-two specific political and civic activities during the previous year, other than voting or discussing politics. Those endeavors ranged from the most common activities (e.g., 35 percent worked with others to solve a community problem, 22 percent attended a political meeting about local concerns, 22 percent signed a physical petition) to a variety of infrequent acts of participation (e.g., only 3 percent sent a letter to the editor of a newspaper or magazine by physical mail, 4 percent did so digitally, and 6 percent attended an organized protest gathering). In total, a majority of Americans were involved in two or more of those activities. Although young adults are somewhat less likely to be physically involved in the political process, they are more likely than others to get engaged through digital means—a route undertaken by nearly two-thirds of those in the eighteen-to-twenty-four age group.[6]

Pew's research also revealed that the people who are most ideologically consistent in their views—and thus probably clearer and perhaps more mature in their political ruminations—are considerably more active in political affairs than those who hold milder points of view. For instance, those who are either consistently liberal or consistently conservative are twice as likely as citizens with more moderate views to donate money and attend campaign events, and are at least 50 percent more likely to contact elected officials and volunteer to help a candidate or campaign. The consistent ideologues are also substantially more likely to vote.[7] Unfortunately, as we will see in a subsequent chapter on ideological standing, a large share of Americans resides in the "mushy middle" of political ideology.

Another variable that comes into play is the complexity of our world. No issue exists in isolation from other issues. Every individual is affected by the needs, preferences, and behavior of every other. Making sense of reality has become exceedingly difficult. The media's influence is a direct result of people's desire to be in touch with the world around them, without having the capacity to be everywhere at once and experience all that is happening. Given the information filtered through the media, and their personal proclivities, many people simplify the world by adopting a single issue as their bell-wether for understanding and having personal impact. Single-issue politics becomes the channel through which millions of Americans balance political participation with the performance of their day-to-day responsibilities.

Key Facts

- 35 percent of the voting-eligible population in the United States is not registered to vote. That represents more than 85 million people who have chosen not to participate.[8]
- In the general elections for the four presidential elections since 2000, 59.2 percent of adults who were eligible to vote actually did so.[9]
- Turnout was 39.2 percent in the most recent pair of midterm elections.[10]
- In presidential primaries, turnout varies by state. In statewide primaries during 2008 and 2012, primary turnout has ranged from just 1 percent of registered voters to barely more than half.[11]
- During the last two presidential election cycles (2012, 2008), average turnout in the primary elections was 15 percent.[12]
- During the four midterm elections since 2000, average voter turnout in the general elections has been 40 percent of all voting-eligible adults.[13]
- 72 percent of adults have been involved in one or more political and civic activities during the previous year, other than voting

or discussing politics. The most common effort was working with others to solve a community problem (35 percent).[14]

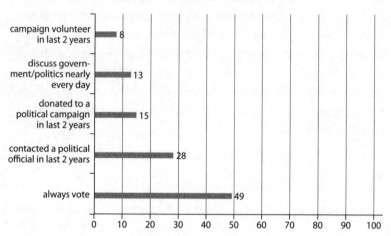

Political Engagement Activities

Source: Pew Research Center, Political Polarization in the American Public, June 2014, N=10,013.

Outlook and Interpretation

One could easily make the argument that the importance of socio-political engagement gets shortchanged. America's culture war exists because various segments of the public are committed to championing issues that go a long way toward defining American culture. The outcome of that war will be determined by how many people engage in the tussle and which positions they take. The future of American culture will not be dictated by the silent masses that clog the sidelines.

One of the most important rights a citizen has is the right to vote. Why don't more Americans vote? Why don't people exercise the opportunity to influence their own future and that of the country, a privilege that several billion people around the world would love to have?

84

Understanding people's tendency to avoid that responsibility is complicated. Research shows that some of the most common reasons include sheer disinterest or distrust in politics or the election; forgetting the date of the election; not registering in time to vote; disliking the candidates on the ballot; not knowing where the voting place is located; feeling as if their vote does not make a difference; taking the privilege for granted; and feeling inadequately educated about the candidates and issues. However, recent innovations, such as same-day registration (a growing option but not available in all states), absentee ballots, and extended voting periods (i.e., voting is possible on multiple days, not just on Election Day), are eliminating some of the most frequent excuses.[15]

In reality, deeper issues lie behind people's ambivalence about political participation. One has been the relatively recent failure of public schools to promote civic understanding and responsibility among young people. Another is the tenor of political conversation advanced through mass media, which seeks to stir controversy and focuses on conflict rather than substantive content and finding common ground. Furthermore, millions of Americans frankly admit they are so busy pursuing personal interests that they devote little attention to understanding or engaging in the electoral process.

Amid America's prolonged success, comfort, and security, people's sense of obligation to the country and duty to fellow citizens has all but vanished. That development has been aided by the shift in values from seeking the common good to pursuing self-interest. Surveys have shown that a growing proportion of Americans have little sense of duty to participate in governance at any level—national, regional, state, or local—unless there is the promise of some tangible and direct personal benefit. Electing one candidate over another, in most people's minds, does not qualify as providing such an advantage because they don't like, trust, or feel served by most candidates.[16]

Millions of Americans have adopted a "victim mentality," believing the system is beyond their control and they have become little more than pawns in a game played by professional politicians and the media. Unless the public embraces the perspective of the Founding Fathers—that the nation is governed by the people and for the people, and it is the right and responsibility of the public to straighten out the system when it falls prey to abuse—then we will likely continue to see fewer people participate, and the sense of anomie and powerlessness grow.

The Christian Church certainly has a responsibility to educate and motivate people with respect to political participation. Recent efforts by organizations such as United in Purpose, Family Research Council, American Family Association, and Liberty Counsel, among others, have gone a long way toward encouraging churches to understand their rights and opportunities related to challenging Christians to be well-versed and active in relation to national, state, and local governance. In each of the past three election cycles, small but growing numbers of churches have taught their congregants how biblical principles and narratives relate to the issues troubling America today. These initiatives, along with efforts to register congregants to vote, have the potential to begin moving the nation in a better direction.

10
POLITICAL
IDEOLOGY

Summary

Where do we, as a nation, stand ideologically? The answer to that question helps explain why we have such severe public policy gridlock, political animosity, voting ambivalence, and relational friction.

The nation's ideological profile is constantly shifting, albeit not as dramatically as some pundits might believe. In fact, from 2004 to 2014, the changes were minor in scope. While the percentage of self-identified conservatives remained constant (about 37 percent), the proportion of liberals increased by several points (to roughly 25 percent), mostly at the expense of moderates (who shrunk by about four points, to 35 percent).[1]

Not surprisingly, Democrats are the party most likely to attract liberals. Not quite half of all Democrats (44 percent) consider themselves to be liberal, which is more than double the percentage of liberals found among Independents and nine times as many as are aligned with the GOP. Stated differently, almost two-thirds of all liberals (63 percent) are Democrats, while 30 percent are Independent, and only 7 percent are Republican.[2]

In contrast, most Republicans lean to the right; 70 percent of adults associated with the GOP call themselves conservative. Compared to liberals, conservatives are more broadly distributed across the three parties—57 percent Republican, 27 percent Independent, and 16 percent Democrat—but the GOP remains the most common landing spot for conservatives.[3]

Moderates are almost equally as likely to be Democrats (36 percent) as they are to be Independent (41 percent), with only one-quarter claiming a Republican affiliation.[4]

The change pattern over the last decade is instructive. The proportion of Democrats who are self-professed liberals has grown by eleven points in the past decade. Meanwhile, the proportion of Republicans who say they are conservative has remained stable in the last ten years. The proportion of moderates has decreased among all three voter groups (i.e., Democrat, Republican, and Independent) during the past decade.[5]

Survey after survey identifies the low esteem in which voters hold the two major political parties. Even though seven out of ten registered voters are aligned with one of the two major parties, fewer than half of all Americans have held a positive view of those parties during the past several years.[6] Yet, Americans have become highly partisan in their outlook, even though they are not fully onboard with the candidates and policies supported by their party of choice. That partisan perspective has facilitated the growing animosity toward people who hold different views or side with a different party.

Being conservative or liberal in one dimension of public policy does not always predict a similar ideological position in other dimensions. For instance, one series of studies revealed that many adults have a divided mind when it comes to sociopolitical ideology. Approximately one out of every ten who described themselves as conservative, and about two out of every ten who claimed to be liberal, also admitted that they had ideologically opposite views on a number of different issues.[7] Another study by Pew reported that people's views are becoming more consistent, and yet four out of ten adults harbor mixed ideological views.[8]

Other research has confirmed the ideological inconsistency existent today. For instance, drawing on data from four recent Pew studies, 15 percent of those who identified as either conservative or liberal then embraced positions on at least one of seven issues that did not jibe with their ideological position. For example, 16 percent of self-identified conservatives said they supported legalized abortion in all situations; 16 percent opposed defunding Planned Parenthood; one in ten rejected the idea that gun ownership protects people; 15 percent opposed protecting the right to own guns; and 8 percent said they were satisfied with the performance of the federal government. Among the respondents who said they were liberal, 20 percent agreed that gun ownership helps protect people; 21 percent claimed that reasons other than human activity explain changes in the climate; and 16 percent opposed the legalization of abortion.[9]

Conflicting patterns are evident in the nation. On the one hand, our country is getting older, on average, and Americans tend to become more conservative with age. That is partially a reflection of their enhanced socioeconomic status and the related desire to protect what they have earned. It also reflects a different upbringing regarding the importance of freedom, what it takes to protect our freedoms, and divergent emotions about the nation itself. On the other hand, two younger generations (Millennials and Gen Xers) have been more liberal than the older generations for the past twenty years, with no sign on the horizon of meaningful change in that pattern. The culture war is, therefore, partially explained by the older, more conservative Americans hanging on to traditional views and values, while the upcoming younger folks push and prod to loosen up the nation's moral and political standards.[10]

Key Facts

Party Identification and Ideology

	Conservative	Liberal
All adults	38%	24%
Democrats	16	63
Republicans	57	7
Independents	27	30

Source: Gallup Organization, January 2015, N=16,479 adults 18 or older.[*]

*http://fivethirtyeight.com/datalab/there-are-more-liberals-but-not-fewer-conservatives/; http://www.gallup.com/poll/180452/liberals-record-trail-conservatives.aspx.

Generational Ideology, Based on Self-Description

Generation	Cohort	Conservative	Moderate	Liberal	Conservative–Liberal Gap
Millennials	1980–1996	28%	40%	30%	- 2 percentage points
Generation X	1965–1979	35	39	23	+12
Baby Boom	1946–1964	44	33	21	+23
Elders	1900–1945	48	33	17	+31
All adults		38	36	24	+14

Source: Gallup Organization, January 2015, N=16,479 adults 18 or older.[**]

**http://www.gallup.com/poll/181325/baby-boomers-likely-identify-conservative.aspx?g_source=.

Outlook and Interpretation

Three things are clear about people's ideological views. First, a growing share of the population is becoming more liberal. It seems that ideological preferences have typically been part of a pendulum swing that stray a bit from the center, either to the left or right, but never get too extreme. As a nation, we tend to be moderate in our views, typically leaning toward one end or the other of the ideological continuum. Currently, most people lean somewhat to the right, but the momentum appears to be shifting leftward, thanks to changes in demographics and worldview.

**American Political
Ideology Regarding Social
and Economic Issues**

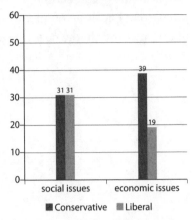

Source: Gallup Organization, N=1,024, May 2015.

Second, Americans are not ideological purists. One significant reason for the ideological confusion and inconsistency that prevail in America today—apart from the labels people embrace—is that we no longer possess an anchor for truth. In contemporary America, truth is whatever we say it is. We have adopted the mind-set that everyone must determine their own truth, and nobody can legitimately question the veracity of that perspective for that individual. The notion of embracing absolutes is anathema to most Americans. Unchanging standards are a blast from the past. Today, everything is up for grabs. Purity is a concept more than a reality.

Finally, because of the complexity of life in this century, and the excessive amount of information hurled at us from every direction and perspective, Americans look for shortcuts. Ideological labels have become one of those shortcuts. It is faster and easier to adopt the "conservative" or "liberal" position than to study an issue and arrive at a position that more accurately reflects who we are and what we believe. The resulting inconsistencies in people's political determinations are partially because of this desire to rely on a simpler way to understand and respond to reality.

It is difficult in America's noisy, contentious political environment to identify the middle-ground position on many issues, and it does not look like it will get any easier in the near future.

11
NATIONAL
PRIORITIES

Summary

Determining the major issues facing the country is important when deciding how national resources will be allocated. As has been evident especially during election campaigns, the "sexy" issues get attention as well as the promise of funding and action. Sadly, many crucial issues that lack public appeal get overlooked or avoided because they are not represented by a powerful or desirable constituency.

But assessing the nation's biggest challenges also depends on people's ideological perspective and how we measure which issues are at the forefront of people's minds. In the end, no matter how we approach it, people's sense of the critical issues facing the nation is both a volatile and important component in understanding the American mind-set.

First, some issues, such as economic realities, matters of governance, and national security, are a constant part of the discussion. They are often included in the discussion because of a convergence of the entities that determine the slate: public officials, media, and voters.[1]

Second, some issues are of widespread concern to Americans but are not "top-of-mind" issues—meaning they do not immediately spring to mind when people are asked to identify their primary concerns about the state of the nation. When people are asked specifically about these issues, however, a different picture emerges, displaying a depth of concern that was not evident using a top-of-mind measurement. Such issues include gun control, abortion, cybersecurity, the cost of college education, and Social Security. People realize these matters are significant to their or the nation's well-being but may not be sufficiently high-profile in their daily activities and patterns to stay ingrained in their thoughts.

Third, some issues are here today but gone tomorrow. Often, these matters rise and fall according to current conditions; as conditions change, the issues appear or disappear from people's radar. Ethics, foreign aid, war, national unity, energy costs, and racism are among the issues in this category. These considerations rarely go away but often become less high-profile or influential for a period of time.

Finally, some matters are of irrefutable significance to the health and well-being of the United States but for a variety of reasons get little, if any, public attention or consideration. Such matters include the water supply, the decline in interpersonal respect, prison reform, national infrastructure rehabilitation, and poverty. Often, these are vexing challenges public officials put off for their successors to address, hoping that by effectively ignoring the issues, it will not come back to harm them politically. Of course, these public servants seem to forget that the nation is invariably harmed by delaying the development and execution of needed solutions.

The top issues Americans usually identify relate to economics (wages, taxes, employment), government performance (budget, ethics, legislative productivity, debt), public safety (terrorism, national defense, police behavior), and personal well-being (Social Security, Medicare, health care, crime).[2]

At the tail end of 2015, for instance, the top-of-mind issues that were the highest priority—that is, issues that immediately came to mind, without any prompting or choices provided—included dissatisfaction with government performance, economic stagnation, and immigration reform. In addition, issues that at least two-thirds of adults selected from a longer list of possibilities included defense against terrorism, strengthening the economy, providing better job options, an improved education system, strengthening the Social Security system, reducing the federal deficit, and lowering health-care costs.[3]

Of course, the issues identified as priorities vary from group to group. For example, Republicans and conservatives are likely to focus on taxes, immigration, terrorism, national defense, morality, and the national debt. Democrats and liberals are usually more concerned about environmental matters, income inequality, the education system, public works, racial tension, and transitioning our energy sources. Are there points of agreement? Perhaps when it comes to identifying a few important issues, although that unity rarely seems to include agreement on the strategies for creating positive change. Those matters of common concern include Medicare reform, employment, global trade policies, crime, economic reform, and strengthening Social Security.[4]

In the same way, a person's age is correlated with the issues they consider most significant. Younger adults are much more likely than older adults to prioritize the educational system and environmental concerns. Middle-aged adults focus on economic priorities, such as poverty, the federal budget deficit, and reigniting the economy. Older adults are most energized about terrorism, infrastructure, immigration, tax reform, Social Security, Medicare, and national defense.[5]

A spiritual component is also associated with our perspective on issues. Evangelicals, for instance, reflect above-average interest in morality, poverty, personal freedom, and government performance and interference. They are consistently less interested in environmental matters.[6]

Key Facts

- When given a list of twenty-three issues and asked to indicate which were considered a top priority for our public officials to solve, the top-rated issues in 2015 were: terrorism (76 percent), the economy (75 percent), jobs (67 percent), education (67 percent), Social Security (66 percent), the federal budget deficit (64 percent), and health-care costs (64 percent).[7]

- The top-rated issues among Republicans were: defending the nation against terrorism (87 percent), improving the economy (75 percent), reducing the federal budget deficit (72 percent), improving the military (71 percent), and improving the job situation (70 percent).[8]

- In contrast, the top-rated issues among Democrats were: improving the educational system (77 percent), improving the economy (72 percent), improving the job situation (72 percent), defending the nation against terrorism (71 percent), reducing health-care costs (70 percent), and addressing poverty (70 percent).[9]

- Independent voters had yet a different schedule of top-rated issues. They included: improving the economy (75 percent), defending the nation against terrorism (74 percent), and strengthening the Social Security system (70 percent).[10]

- Top-of-mind measures of our key issues indicate that those issues are: dissatisfaction with government (16 percent), the state of the economy (13 percent), unemployment and jobs (8 percent), immigration (8 percent), gun control (7 percent), health care (6 percent), federal budget deficit and debt (5 percent), ethics and morals (5 percent), and crime (5 percent).[11]

- Using a top-of-mind measure, evangelicals are more likely than other adults to cite the loss of personal freedom (7 percentage points higher), declining morals (+6 percentage points), and government spending (+5 percentage points) as major national problems. In contrast, evangelicals are only half as likely as other adults to cite environmental issues as serious challenges.[12]

**National Priorities Can Change Dramatically
from Month to Month**

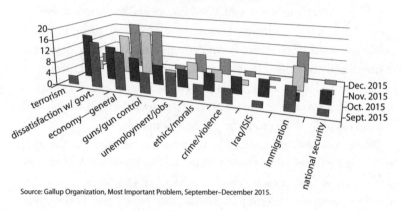

Source: Gallup Organization, Most Important Problem, September–December 2015.

Outlook and Interpretation

During the coming decade, the list of top-ranked national problems will likely change as often as Kim Kardashian's outfits. In this irreversibly interconnected world, it is virtually impossible to predict what people will perceive to be the most pressing issues far in advance; events around the world reshuffle the deck every day, if not multiple times a day. Add to that the countless distractions people face, causing their attention to be diverted from things that matter and rendering their opinions frequently ill-informed and superficial. Further, because people's perceptions and opinions are so dependent on media coverage, evolving conditions, leadership engagement, and their personal circumstances, do not be surprised to be confronted with a revolving pantheon of perceived challenges.

Perhaps the most important factor to consider is which issues are likely to drop from contention among the most serious and which are most likely to join the top-tier concerns. Again, because of the interdependence of nations, forecasting such outcomes is fraught with peril. However, we can make some educated guesses.

For instance, Americans cannot continue to conduct their business and enjoy life if the nation's infrastructure crumbles at its current rate. The American Society of Civil Engineers' most recent evaluation of our national infrastructure wound up awarding us a D+, while the World Economic Forum compared us to other developed nations and concluded that we rank sixteenth in overall infrastructure quality. This is a bigger issue than people realize; it cannot be ignored if we want the United States to remain a vibrant and viable nation capable of meeting the public's demands.[13]

Water is a basic necessity. The water wars that have been gaining momentum in the western states may well become a breakout issue in the near future, as states and municipalities fight for the right to use the decreasing water supply available for public use. This includes forthcoming battles between farms, businesses, and households over the allocation and pricing of water. The decay of our water pipes—for wastewater disposal as well as the delivery of potable water—is another massive challenge we have not solved.

But our water woes are just one of the pressure points that are likely to gain a higher profile as time goes on. Add other serious infrastructure perils—crumbling bridges, outdated and overburdened transportation systems, an inadequate power grid, decrepit inland waterways, insufficient airport capacity, hazardous waste cleanup—and the pressure for action (and funding) will continue to grow. The most recent quadrennial American Society of Civil Engineers' report that surveys our infrastructure needs estimated that we must spend close to 4 trillion dollars by 2020 to bring our systems up to speed.[14]

And although many technology-related challenges loom before us, perhaps the one most likely to join the upper echelon of national concerns is cybersecurity. The growing number of cyber attacks that have made the headlines in the past few years and have crippled the victims whose databases were hacked are just the tip of the iceberg. The public has yet to understand the scope of the dangers posed to their personal security, much less the nation's economy and national defense.

It is not much of a leap of logic to posit that one reason why there is so much division concerning which issues and solutions deserve our resources is because Americans today lack a common vision. Without a unifying thread on which to focus our attention and serve as a point of agreement in moving toward solutions, we splinter into ideological camps and fight over competing visions of an ideal or attainable future. In practice, it is the job of the nation's leaders to develop and champion such a vision. We can only hope we will see more leaders who empower the nation to rally around a shared vision that enables us to invest less energy into bickering and politicking, and more into solving America's problems.

PART 3

LIFESTYLES AND PERSPECTIVES

12
POPULATION
GROWTH

Summary

While nations like China and India explode with growth, the United States continues to plod along at less than 1 percent population growth every year. That may seem minimal, but over the course of the 2011–2020 decade, due to the anticipated 7 percent expansion of a population that stood at 312 million people in 2011, the US population is expected to reach 334 million in 2020. In other words, in America's current state, just 7 percent growth over a decade adds more than 20 million people to the total. In fact, the Census Bureau estimates that given a mixture of factors that affect our rate of growth, the United States is expected to reach 400 million people by 2051. While China and India have left us in the dust population-wise—China's estimated population at the start of 2016 was 1.4 billion and India's was believed to be 1.3 billion—the United States remains the third most populous nation in the world.[1]

Despite that expansion, things have changed dramatically during the past fifty years on the population-boom front. In regard to population growth, many assume such an increase is due to a blossoming number of new births. That is not the case in America. Our fertility rate—the number of children the typical woman has—is just 1.86. That is significant because it takes an average of 2.1 children born per woman to reach "replacement level," meaning the number of live births per woman it takes for a population to maintain its size. America has been substantially below that level for a number of years. Another measure, known as the birthrate, is at just 12.5 children per 1,000 women in the country—the lowest level measured since such records have been maintained.[2] Despite these low levels of childbirth, our population continues to grow. Why? Because of immigration, aging, and to a lesser extent, a slow decline in the number of abortions.

It's not that Americans are failing to produce children. The most famous baby-producing time was just after World War II, when soldiers returned home and we had the infamous Baby Boom. From 1946 to 1964, the population grew like never before. In 1946, for the first time in the nation's history, more than 3 million babies were born in a year. Just eight years later, 1954 claimed the distinction of being the first time 4 million babies were born in a year. At least 4 million children were born each year through 1964, after which we entered a bit of a birth dearth, declining from 4 million births in 1964 to 3.76 million in 1965, until we hit a low of 3.14 million in 1973. The numbers started to slowly climb again until we returned to the 4 million mark in 1989. We have experienced in the neighborhood of 4 million births per year ever since.[3]

However, 4 million births a year is not as impressive now as it was in 1954. Back then, the nation's total population was just half of what it is today. Even in 1989, the nation's population was almost 80 million people smaller than it is today. That means we have more than 30 million additional women of childbearing age in the United States these days, but we are having the same number of live births.

A nation's total population increases for various reasons though. The number of live births is one of them. The prevalence of immigration is another. Expanded longevity is a third reason—one that has affected our country significantly. Globally, life expectancy was 48 years in 1950 and has jumped to 69 years today and is expected to reach 76 by 2050. Longevity is even greater in the United States, thanks to better health care, diets, living conditions, and hygiene. The typical American lived to be 68 in 1950, survives to an average age of 79 today, and should average 84 years by midcentury.[4]

An often-overlooked explanation for population growth also has to do with the shifting religious balance. Some faiths encourage large families; others do not. A nation dominated by a pro-birth faith system, such as Islam or Christianity, typically has a rapidly growing population, conditions permitting. Worldwide, Muslim women have the highest fertility rate, at 3.1, followed by Christian women at 2.7. Buddhist women, who believe in reincarnation and thus have less of a theological motivation to bring new life into the world, are well below the replacement level (1.6), as are those who have no religious inclination and tend to place a lower value on life (1.7).[5]

The United States has also depressed its population growth through abortion. Since the *Roe v. Wade* Supreme Court decision in 1973 that legalized abortion, it is estimated that the United States has permitted 57 million abortions. If all of those babies had been allowed to live, and were a nation of their own, they would represent the twenty-third most-populated nation in the world, about the same size as Italy and England. Their presence in today's population would boost the size of the United States by about one-sixth of its current size.[6]

That tragic loss of life has been numerically offset to a large extent through immigration. Immigrants comprise roughly 13 percent of the population, representing about 41 million people. America welcomes approximately 1 million new immigrants to the country each year, a decline from the levels in the previous decade (when we averaged 1.4 million annually from 2000 through 2010).[7]

Our population actually might have been on the decline if it were not for the higher birthrates among America's ethnic women. While young white women are a declining percentage of the population and also have the lowest birthrate among US females, ethnic women of childbearing age are growing quickly in number. The largest growth is among Hispanics and Asians. By 2060, the Hispanic population as a proportion of the total population is expected to jump by more than 60 percent, to represent close to 30 percent of the total citizenry. The Asian population as a proportion of the total population is expected to explode by more than 80 percent during that same time frame, to bring its overall population proportion to nearly 12 percent.[8]

Generations are also of interest to many cultural observers. The idea of a generation is a sociological fabrication that merely helps us to track what is happening with different age groups within a larger population. The Baby Boomers, of course, have received the lion's share of generational attention over the years because they have been the largest generation in America's history.[9] However, 2015 brought about a change in that reality, as the so-called Millennials took over as the largest generation currently in the United States. Boomers peaked at 78.8 million people in 1999, setting the record, and have fallen to just below 75 million in 2015. Millennials, who are expected to top out around 81.1 million in 2036, were slightly more than 75 million in 2015 and will continue to increase for several years beyond that (thanks to immigration). The generation stuffed in between them, known as Gen X or Baby Busters, is expected to hit its ceiling in 2018, at roughly 65.8 million people.[10]

Key Facts

- The US population has grown every year for more than two centuries. The population at the beginning of each of the last seven decades has been as follows:[11]

1950	151,325,798
1960	179,323,175
1970	203,302,031
1980	226,542,199
1990	248,718,302
2000	281,424,603
2010	308,745,538
2015	323,000,000 (est.)

- The number of live births in the United States in 2014 was 3.98 million. The estimated number of deaths recorded in 2014 was 2.64 million. The net population gain was about 1.3 million people. Immigration adds another million people per year. During the course of this decade, we have had an average growth rate of about 0.76 percent per year.[12]

- The global fertility rates of women aligned with various faith groups is notably different: Muslim (3.1), Christian (2.7), Hindu (2.4), Jewish (2.3), no faith (1.7), and Buddhist (1.6).[13]

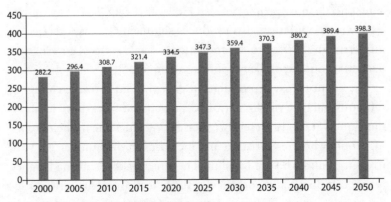

US Population and Projections

(in millions of people)

Source: US Census Bureau, 2014 National Population Projections.

- Since 1973, the United States has allowed an estimated 57 million abortions. The greatest number of abortions in a year was in 1990, when 1.61 million children were aborted. The number appears to have been in a slow but steady decline since 2008.[14]
- After a decade of averaging 1.4 million immigrants per year (2000–2010), current immigration levels average about 1 million people annually.[15]
- The number of people sixty-five or older will jump from 48 million in 2015 to 74 million in 2030—a 54 percent increase in only fifteen years![16]

Outlook and Interpretation

While a simple count of the number of people residing on a land mass such as the United States might seem innocuous, hidden behind the final statistic are some politically explosive realities.

An increasing population is often perceived to be a positive condition. It is thought to reflect a nation whose people are enjoying sexual expression, family experiences, and the financial wherewithal to sustain those lives. Economists note that a growing population facilitates a healthier economy because of the increased level of consumer needs those people possess. However, beyond a certain point, a growing population also produces significant stresses related to infrastructure, safety, food production, social services, governance, natural resources, and environmental impact.

The silent threat of population growth relates to the changing religious balance of the nation. As discussed in earlier chapters, the United States is presently experiencing a decline in the number of people who are Christian and increases in the number who are irreligious and who are Muslim. The effect of this shifting balance is that our dominant worldview is likely to shift along with our religious alignments. The rapid growth of those who are religiously disinclined points to a nation likely to produce fewer births in total. That likelihood is supported by the plummeting interest in having children among young American women. Add to that the consistent growth of a group with the highest fertility rate and a dramatically divergent worldview (i.e., Muslims), while the Christian population shrinks due to both a declining fertility rate and fewer converts. Mix it all together and the result is a national worldview that is morphing away from a traditional biblical perspective toward something yet to be determined but certainly vastly different from America's historical outlook and values.

The sub-replacement level birthrate and reliance on immigration for population increase also suggests that the median age of the population will continue to rise. An aging population brings a different set of needs to the table, especially in terms of factors such as health care and residential choices.

The generational data also remind us that our nation is getting older, while most of the world is getting younger. In the next fifteen years, the proportion of our population under eighteen will decline by almost two percentage points, while the percentage who are sixty-five or older will rise by 5.6 points. That's a big swing in a short period. It suggests that there will be structural changes in how our country operates, as the needs shift away from elementary schools and more toward senior care centers (as just one of dozens of examples).

Despite these considerations, the bottom line is that our population is likely to continue growing at a slow but sustainable pace. The nation's population was about 323 million at the end of 2015 and is expected to reach 335 million by 2020, 359 million in 2030, 380 million in 2040, and just shy of 400 million by the middle of this century. It may not be the robust rate of growth we have historically experienced, but it represents growth and all of the opportunities and challenges that come with it.

13
HAPPINESS

Summary

How do you quantify happiness? What are the appropriate metrics for determining the overall happiness of a nation? Ask a dozen researchers and you'll likely get a dozen distinct sets of measures. (That's not hyperbole—I examined the happiness measures used by twelve independent research groups and discovered overlapping but unique approaches to determining happiness.)[1]

But researchers have now spent several decades testing different theories and measurements, producing some good insights and useful measures. The statistical outcomes vary somewhat—probably due to differences in question wording and sequencing, sampling methodology, and data collection modes—but the data patterns and general conclusions are strikingly similar.

The emerging narrative explains that culture matters a great deal: what facilitates happiness in the United States is different from what contributes to similar outcomes in other nations. When the overall happiness of Americans is compared to that of people in other nations, we typically rank in the second tier of nations; we invariably place outside the top ten countries, regardless of which nations or how many are included in the study. (For what it's worth, people living in the Scandinavian nations—Denmark, Norway, Sweden, Finland, Iceland—consistently rate among the most contented people on Earth, no matter how researchers measure happiness.)

Further, the body of research suggests that most Americans would describe themselves as generally happy but not completely so. Somewhere between one-fifth and one-third of us would label ourselves "very happy," while a somewhat larger share of us would say we are "somewhat happy." In general, levels of happiness have been on a slow decline for several years and seem likely to continue that slump unless some significant culture changes occur. These studies also indicate that our sense of happiness can vary dramatically from day to day, and certainly from month to month. It is not unusual for there to be swings of ten to fifteen percentage points in self-reported happiness levels when comparing survey outcomes conducted during the same week from year to year.

More importantly, numerous factors contribute to our sense of happiness, but each person weighs those factors in a unique and complex manner. However, the accumulated research shows there are identifiable factors that seem indispensable for Americans to feel happy. Those factors include: being married, employed, and relatively wealthy; having sufficient positive and supportive relationships and good mental health; actively engaging in religious belief and behavior; experiencing a high degree of trust in people; and having the freedom to make choices. It also seems that possessing a growing sense of optimism about the future causes us to adopt a heightened sense of happiness. (Currently, Americans are more likely to believe in the future than to be pleased about their present.)

Factors that do not have as much positive effect on our happiness include: personal accomplishments, intense engagement, substantial leisure activity, and extensive economic assets.

However, identifying the factors that seem to have an impact on our happiness does not mean we can easily and directly influence those factors and thus improve our perspective on life. For instance, one of the influential components related to feeling happy is the state of the economy. When the economy is good or getting stronger, our sense of well-being tends to rise; when it is declining or doing poorly, our happiness is more likely to suffer. However, the future state of the economy is neither highly predictable nor easily influenced. Just ask recent presidents about the latter and check out the track record of professional economists, much less citizens at large, on the former!

Similarly, incorporating components that correlate with happiness into one's life does not guarantee inner sunshine. After all, there is a positive correlation between wealth and happiness. Yet, research has also revealed that stockpiling money doesn't necessarily improve a person's life outlook. One recent survey of megamillionaires (i.e., households with at least $25 million in assets), sponsored by the Bill & Melinda Gates Foundation, revealed that people with great wealth are a fearful and worried bunch, with such anxieties often caused by the pressure and challenges of their fortunes. That study reported that many of the super-wealthy people experienced heightened happiness only when they began to give away large chunks of their wealth—effectively reducing the outsized responsibilities and concerns that accompanied that wealth. Another study that tested the relationship between money and happiness concluded that happiness increases along with income, but only up to a point. In America, that point appears to be roughly $75,000 per year (per household), after which one's happiness is not enhanced by more money (but may be increased by other resources, conditions, or experiences that are enabled by money).[2]

Happiness and satisfaction with life seem related to life cycles. For instance, young adults and the elderly are generally the happiest and most satisfied individuals. People in their late forties through midfifties generally experience a decrease in happiness.

Key Facts

Drawing on measures that seem to be most representative of the breadth of happiness ratings available, here are some important highlights:

- Roughly one-third of Americans (33 percent) consider themselves to be very happy.[3] In general, about seven out of ten Americans are likely to say they are "happy."[4]

- Daily mood tracking shows that our degree of happiness swings up and down quite freely. At the time of this writing, 46 percent of US adults had "a lot of happiness and enjoyment," while 10 percent had "a lot of stress and worry."[5]

- The primary contributors to personal happiness include: watching your children or grandchildren succeed (72 percent); kissing or hugging someone you love (72 percent); being told you are a person who can be trusted or relied on (69 percent); spending time with family or friends (69 percent); experiencing a special moment with a child (64 percent); enjoying natural beauty, like a sunset or the ocean (61 percent); hearing or seeing something funny that makes you laugh (60 percent).[6]

Positive Experience Index Score, Selected Nations

81+	79–80	76–78	72–75	65–71	56–64	45–55
Paraguay	Singapore	Denmark	Australia	India	Uganda	Afghanistan
Colombia	Switzerland	Germany	China	Japan	Haiti	Nepal
Ecuador	Argentina	France	United Kingdom	Russia	Israel	Bangladesh
Guatemala	Canada	Mexico	Brazil	Italy	Iraq	Serbia
Panama	Netherlands	Finland	Spain	Poland	S. Korea	Turkey
Costa Rica	New Zealand	Kenya	Saudi Arabia	Jamaica	Egypt	Tunisia
Venezuela	United States	Ireland	Portugal	Jordan	Pakistan	Sudan

Positive experiences defined as these past-day experiences: well-rested, consistently respected, laughed a lot, experienced something interesting, felt a lot of enjoyment. Global mean: 71; US mean: 79. Source: Gallup Organization, Positive Experience Index Score, 2014. Published March 19, 2015, http://www.gallup.com/poll/182009/mood-world-upbeat-international-happiness-day.aspx?g_source=happiness&g_medium=search&g_campaign=tiles.

Outlook and Interpretation

From a purely social scientific perspective, the temptation is to predict a prolonged period of declining happiness. Based on the factors that correlate most closely with joy, the coming five years or so do not give rise to optimism. Based on the factors that a variety of studies have discovered are most likely to produce happiness, we find:

- Fewer people are having children, and those who have them are bearing fewer of them.
- Americans are experiencing fewer close and lasting personal relationships.
- Adults are less likely to devote time to God and to the Bible, and those who do invest time in these pursuits are spending less time with God and His Word.
- A declining proportion of households are experiencing financial freedom at the same time that government regulations and significant shifts in business strategy are limiting growth in personal earnings and asset development.
- The number of Americans suffering from mental illnesses and physical limitations is on the rise.
- People have a declining sense of trust and confidence in both individuals and institutions.

What, then, might turn around these challenges and enable more Americans to experience heightened levels of happiness? The research offers some strong possibilities:

- Changed attitudes about children, parenting, and family.
- Less reliance on technology for communications and interaction and greater emphasis on face-to-face relationships.
- A deeper personal commitment to faith in God and a renewed interest in corporate expressions of faith.

- A national and global economy that is growing at a healthy pace and is welcoming more people into fulfilling jobs and higher earnings.
- Superior care given to those who suffer from mental and physical handicaps.
- The restoration of traditional values that facilitate a greater sense of trust in people and institutions.

Even just a few of these gains would support a substantial turnaround in the national happiness quotient. While it is possible that some type of economic recovery could emerge, the chances of seeing several of the other changes also emerge are less hopeful. If anything, it appears that our culture is rapidly moving away from most of these changes.

Our research does reveal that Americans who are more intensely involved in following Jesus Christ—as measured by Bible reading, church attendance, regular prayer, participation in Christian education classes, and acts of outreach and service—are typically happier than are nonreligious adults. That should not be a surprise since Christians have more reason than anyone to be happy: we have the guarantee of a blessed eternal life in the presence of a loving Father. One of the visible outcomes of such a relationship with God is joy—not because of what we have accomplished on this earth but due to the grace we receive and the presence of God's Holy Spirit in our lives.[7]

14
LIFE
SATISFACTION

Summary

Americans are a demanding people, but for the most part, they are relatively satisfied with their quality of life. About four out of five Americans (82 percent) say they are satisfied with the overall quality of their life. That perspective has remained rather stable throughout the past decade.

That consistency in outlook is perhaps attributable to the wide range of factors Americans consider when describing their quality of life. The components involved in their mental calculations include how they perceive and feel about personal relationships, cultural health, government performance, financial realities, physical well-being, and the life conditions in which they live. Not surprisingly, individuals assign different degrees of importance to those factors to develop their own unique satisfaction formulas.

The data suggest that Americans maintain a posture of resilient optimism about life. Well aware that deplorable things are happening all around them and that they often are unable to get their way, they nevertheless remain cognizant of their many blessings and stay hopeful that they will use their personal resources—relationships, education, experience, and opportunities—to improve their lot in life.

Americans are currently most comfortable with their physical well-being and the aggregate life conditions they experience. They are somewhat less pleased with the state of their relationships and the performance of government agencies and officials. They are least satisfied with the health of society and the state of the economy. When blended together, most adults come away feeling as if life is far from perfect but is generally treating them well.

- Culturally, adults are most comfortable with how the nation handles crime, with about half satisfied. However, only half as many adults—just 26 percent—say they are satisfied with how the nation is handling issues related to poverty.
- Among the life conditions studied, adults are most pleased with the opportunities to get ahead that are available to them; six out of ten (60 percent) are satisfied with their options. However, only half as many are satisfied with the fairness of income and wealth distribution in America.
- Of the various services the government provides, people seem most at ease with the state and strength of the military. Overall, they are least satisfied with how much it costs the average taxpayer to pay for government services.

Two important limitations on people's optimism, however, are the state of the economy and their personal health. An undeniable correlation exists between people's perceptions of those two factors and their assessment of their life situation. Life satisfaction is most likely to rise when people have the ability to earn a livable income and to feel personally healthy and cared for.[1]

Gallup Organization uses a different set of measures and scores to estimate life satisfaction in more than 135 nations around the world. To put the United States data in context, the Gallup approach suggests that the United States ranks twelfth in overall perceived well-being.[2] That overall ranking is based on five combined measures of well-being:

social well-being (in which the United States ranks fifteenth), sense of purpose (eighteenth), financial well-being (twenty-first), physical well-being (twenty-fifth), and community well-being (twenty-fifth). Notice that the highest categorical rank is fifteenth, yet the aggregate national ranking is twelfth. That means America's combination of factors fares better than is true for most countries. By the way, Panama was the top-rated country in terms of aggregate well-being, taking the top rating in four of the five categories! The tiny Central American nation was distantly trailed in the ratings by Costa Rica and then Denmark.

Key Facts

Overall life satisfaction among US adults: 82 percent.
  Categorical satisfaction scores:

Categories	2015	Change Since 2005	Number of Measures Used
Physical health	71%	n/a	3 measures
Life conditions	53%	no change	8 measures
Relational health	46%	no change	4 measures
Government performance	44%	decreased satisfaction	8 measures
Cultural health	37%	decreased satisfaction	6 measures
Economic health	35%	decreased satisfaction	5 measures

Source: Kim Painter, "USA is Twelfth, Panama First, in Global Well-Being Poll," *USA Today*, September 16, 2014, http://www.usatoday.com/story/news/nation/2014/09/16/global-well-being-poll-panama/15679637/.

Elements of US Well-Being

Measure of Well-Being	US Average	Highest-Ranking State	Lowest-Ranking State
No health insurance	14%	Texas—24%	Massachusetts—5%
Frequently exercise	52%	Alaska—64%	West Virginia—45%
Eat produce frequently	58%	Vermont—64%	Indiana—53%
Recognized for helping community	19%	Alaska—28%	Indiana—17%
Feel active and productive	68%	Wyoming—74%	West Virginia—57%
Worried about money	36%	South Carolina—40%	Wyoming—29%

Source: Gallup Organization, States of the States, December 2015, http://www.gallup.com/poll/125066/State-States.aspx?g_source=CATEGORY_WELLBEING&g_medium=topic&g_.

118

Outlook and Interpretation

If the two most influential factors contributing to the aggregate life satisfaction of Americans relate to economics and physical well-being, then there is reason to be concerned.

Economically, the United States has not fully rebounded—financially or psychologically—from the economic recession that began in 2006. In real dollars, average annual income has not increased in more than a decade, effectively reducing people's buying power as inflation and other costs have risen. Despite happy talk from the federal government, gains reported by various federal agencies in employment and other measures are attributable to changes in reporting or sleight-of-hand analysis more than to actual improvements in the number of jobs, the quality of those jobs, increases in wages and salaries earned, or needed structural changes in the economy. The political gridlock and hyper-partisan quibbling that has paralyzed the nation since the 2004 election has prevented genuine economic progress at the scale required to get America back on track.

Physical well-being is also a dimension in which the potential downside outweighs the likely upside. Medical research is responsible for dramatic breakthroughs in understanding and treating people's physical ailments. However, the cost of health care has spiraled out of control. Thousands of Americans who have serious medical needs are now flying overseas, to nations such as India, to get high-quality medical care at a substantially lower cost than is available to them (even through their health insurance) in the United States.

With a population that is aging, living longer, eating less healthy (e.g., record numbers of obese people—currently north of one-quarter of adults), minimally engaged in helpful exercise, and experiencing increasing health-care costs, the coming years are going to be challenging.

Just as we expect to see the nation's happiness quotient head south, it is likely that we will experience concurrent erosion in overall life satisfaction over the next decade.

15
SUCCESS

Summary

As Americans' lifestyles become more complex, so do their perceptions of what it means to be successful. However, although everyone has their own customized definition of success, most people's perspectives encompass a common core of ideals.

The traditional view has always held that success is about power, possessions, and prestige. The dream life revolved around owning a house in a safe and desirable neighborhood, driving a reliable car, and holding down a steady and good-paying job. It related to having a stellar reputation and attending a respectable church. It incorporated raising healthy and happy children with a loving spouse in a nation that provided freedom and security. Success intrinsically meant the future would be even better than the present because the individual lived in an environment that enabled progress and fulfillment.

To a large extent, those ideals no longer define a successful life. In some cases it is because people take for granted those elements, such as owning a home, living in a free country, or having opportunities in every dimension of life. In other instances, it is because people no longer believe such an outcome is plausible (e.g., the future will be better than the past) or desirable (e.g., regularly attending a church or having children).

Success has a new look. The most pervasive elements in the current success formula are achieving personal goals; having good relationships with family and friends; loving what you do for a living; balancing work, family, and leisure; having ample flexibility; experiencing financial stability; and making a positive difference in the world.[1]

Researchers, however, have added a few pieces to the puzzle, citing components of success people often ignore. The personal traits recognized as contributing factors include consistent and deliberate practice that develops knowledge and skills, resulting in expertise; self-control; grit; and time invested in working hard. It turns out that a few external factors empower success as well. Those include having a competent mentor and intense engagement in a breadth of activities and relationships.[2]

Recent studies indicate that increasing numbers of people are turning to technology to facilitate their personal success, especially when it comes to experiencing a balanced life. People are relying on technological solutions to enable scheduling flexibility, expand the dimensions of the workplace, foster better communication, and increase personal efficiency (which both improves performance and frees up time).[3]

Christians place a high degree of importance on factors such as a strong family unit and a strong relationship with God. However, faith factors have become less prominent in the pursuit of success than matters related to personal achievement, pleasurable experiences, and influence. The only faith group to prioritize faith factors in its definition of success was evangelicals. For that small segment of the population (they are about 7 percent of American adults), nearly nine out of ten individuals identified faith development as crucial to experiencing success.[4]

Success is generally thought to be blocked by economic instability and inflation; the absence of ample opportunities to get ahead and determine one's own future; and the lack of options for affordable education and training.

Key Facts

- 90 percent of American adults believe success is more about happiness than power, possessions, or prestige.[5]
- Among working professionals, 56 percent cited work-life balance as critical to career success, topping the portion of those who cited money (46 percent), recognition (42 percent), or autonomy (42 percent).[6]
- 70 percent of professionals believe they can "have it all"—a successful career and a successful life outside of work—though half believe they may not experience both at the same time.[7]
- Success is largely attributed to achieving personal goals (67 percent); having good relationships with family and friends (66 percent); and loving what you do for a living (60 percent). Only one in five adults (20 percent) says financial wealth defines success.[8]
- 77 percent of professionals believe technology facilitates schedule flexibility, which is important because 80 percent of professionals say flexibility is critical to achieving work-life balance.[9]

Outlook and Interpretation

It seems likely that Americans will find personal success to be increasingly elusive over the coming decade.

As noted in the previous chapter, the replacement of the traditional American Dream with the New Millennium Dream has removed the necessary cornerstones for true success, whether evaluated according

Most Important Outcome for Having a Successful Life

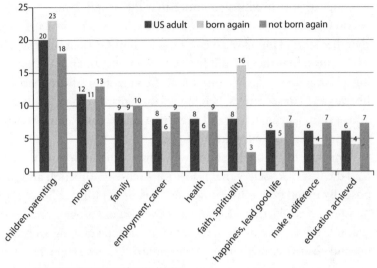

Source: Barna Group, nationwide survey, N=1,004.

to traditional measures or public expectations. The new Dream seeks success through comfort, convenience, choices, connections, entitlement, and experiences. None of those components are evil. However, the combination of them, pursued to the exclusion of the factors expected to produce success (such as painstaking practice and substantial time investment or personal grit and diligence) suggests that many Americans expect to enjoy success without making the challenging personal investments required for it to happen. Further, it is also troubling that adults are increasingly likely to define life balance as meaning less career investment in favor of a more expansive leisure life.

In practice, perceived success most often comes from building up expertise and stability in both work and personal-life endeavors. The discovery that more and more Americans are committed to pursuing their current interests, at the expense of sticking with a particular occupation that produces a solid long-term career, adds weight to the argument that success may not develop as frequently as anticipated.

Don't be surprised if you notice that the people around you are becoming more frustrated with their lack of perceived success and that they start blaming various entities for limiting their success. The assumption that they would have done better if their path had not been blocked will likely cause intensified ideological rifts between liberals and conservatives, heightened disapproval of public officials and government agencies, and a renewed campaign to extract solace from more extensive leisure pursuits.

Amid the drama, Christians will have a golden opportunity to lead the way in a society that is losing its sense of direction and purpose. By quietly demonstrating the value of deploying the historic "Protestant work ethic," followers of Jesus would provide a valuable example for the rest of the nation to follow while making an enduring and positive contribution to the country's future. Unfortunately, assuming that current attitudinal and behavioral patterns persist, it is more likely that Christians will follow rather than lead in this regard and accept the dominant perspectives on success and the most common and popular path thought to lead to success. In other words, Christians are more likely to settle for the dominant cultural alternative rather than heed biblical exhortations to work as if they are serving God Himself and thereby realize success through obedience to His commands and principles. In doing so, Christians are in danger of both dishonoring God and failing American society.[10]

16
MORALITY

Summary

Our moral perspectives are a direct result of our worldview, which is founded on our religious beliefs. Morals are, in essence, the choices we consider to be appropriate. For the first two hundred years or so of America's existence, its people based their moral choices on the truths conveyed in the Bible. In fact, until the start of this millennium, Americans' moral views were predictably stable: because morals were intimately tied to biblical principles, there was no reason for moral moorings to shift. As long as the Bible remained the source from which people's views were drawn, moral standards were set in stone. Desires and behaviors might change but not the standard against which such desires and actions would be judged.

Now, however, people's morals are linked to a different anchor: feelings. As a result, in the past decade or so people's views on morality have changed substantially. The patterns are clear. Adults have become more accepting of twelve of the fifteen moral behaviors surveyed, less accepting of one (having an abortion), and have not changed their views on the other two. Overall, a majority of adults accept eight of the fifteen behaviors as morally acceptable, compared to just five of them a decade ago. The behaviors that have become more acceptable are gay or lesbian relations, having a sexual relationship with someone of the opposite sex to whom one is not married, and doctor-assisted suicide.[1]

It should be noted that all fifteen of the behaviors evaluated run counter to biblical principles.

The behaviors accepted by a majority of Americans include divorce (deemed morally acceptable to 71 percent); sex between an unmarried man and unmarried woman (68 percent); cohabitation (63 percent); enjoying sexual thoughts or fantasies about someone other than a spouse (63 percent); gay or lesbian relations (63 percent); having a baby outside of marriage (61 percent); doctor-assisted suicide (56 percent); and having a sexual relationship with someone of the opposite sex to whom you are not married (53 percent).[2]

Another interesting pattern in the data is that while millions of born-again Christians accept behaviors as morally appropriate that are condemned in the Bible, the born-again constituency has not changed its views nearly as dramatically as the rest of the nation has in the past ten years. For instance, among the non-born-again population, six of the eight behaviors tracked during the past decade experienced a significant increase in acceptance. For the same eight behaviors, the only one to increase significantly in acceptance among born-again Christians was using drugs not prescribed by a medical doctor. Among the born-again segment, three of the behaviors exhibited a decrease in acceptance: cohabitation (embraced by 35 percent but down seven percentage points in the past decade); having an abortion (accepted by one out of seven, which is half as many as a decade ago); and intentionally viewing pornography (currently acceptable to one out of five but down five percentage points).[3]

Summarized differently, these patterns indicate that born-again Christians are generally standing pat morally while the rest of the culture moves toward a more liberal view of morality.

In light of these changes, it is not surprising to learn that two-thirds of all adults say they are concerned about America's moral condition. However, that is a considerable decline in the past decade from the more than four out of five adults who were concerned (a drop from 83 percent to 68 percent). The decline in concern also has affected born-again adults. The proportion of Christ followers expressing concern has dropped from 93 percent to 83 percent.[4]

In general, Americans are aware that the nation's moral values are abysmal—although their assessment of those values has remained unchanged in the past decade. Only one out of five adults (19 percent) has a positive evaluation of the nation's values, while four out of five (79 percent) have a negative view. Those statistics are exactly the same as the figures recorded a decade ago. By more than a three-to-one margin, adults contend that people's morals are getting worse (72 percent) rather than improving (22 percent). Very few Americans argue that morality is not undergoing transition (4 percent). However, these figures also reflect the perspective of Americans a decade ago, suggesting that we may be aware of the moral decay of our society but are not willing to do anything about it.[5]

Key Facts

Moral Acceptability of Behaviors

Activity	All US Adults		Born Again	
	2003	2013/14	2003	2013/14
Cohabitation (living with someone of the opposite sex without being married to them)	60%	63%	42%	35%
Enjoying sexual thoughts or fantasies about someone	59	63	43	42
Having an abortion	45	41	28	14
Having a sexual relationship with someone of the opposite sex to whom you are not married	42	53	30	28
Intentionally looking at pictures that display nudity or explicit sexual behavior	38	43	24	19
Using profanity	36	44	25	22
Getting drunk	35	34	21	19
Using drugs not prescribed by a medical doctor	17	27	11	20

Sources: Research by the Barna Group, Ventura, CA. Studies include OmniPoll 2-03, N=1,024, September 2003; Omni-Poll Frames, N=1,005, June 2013; and OmniPoll 1-14, N=1,024, February 2014.

Activity	All US Adults	
	2005	2015
Divorce	66%	71%
Sex between an unmarried man and unmarried woman	58	68
Having a baby outside of marriage	54	61
Doctor-assisted suicide	49	56
Gay or lesbian relations	44	63
Suicide	13	19
Polygamy (a married person having more than one spouse at a time)	6	16

Sources: Research by the Gallup Organization, Princeton, NJ. Studies conducted in May 2005 (N=1,005) and May 2015 (N=1,024), http://www.gallup.com/poll/16318/societys-moral-boundaries-expand-somewhat-year.aspx; http://www.gallup.com/poll/183413/americans-continue-shift-left-key-moral-issues.aspx.

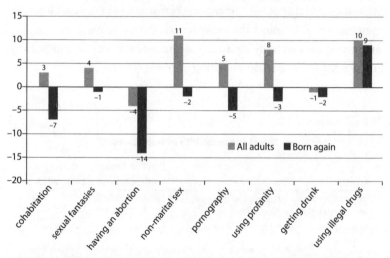

Net Change in Percentage Who Deem a Behavior to be Morally Acceptable, 2003–2013

Source: Barna Group, OmniPoll 2-03, N=1,024, September 2003; OmniPoll Frames, N=1,005, June 2013; and OmniPoll 1-14, N=1,024, February 2014.

Outlook and Interpretation

America's moral condition could move in any of three directions. It could revert to a more traditional Judeo-Christian moral understanding, with our behavior following suit. It could continue to move

128

toward an unapologetically postmodern view of morality, in which we make our own choices independently, with our behavior following suit. Or we could stand pat.

Momentum is currently on the side of unabashedly embracing postmodern morality. As we examine people's priorities to determine the likelihood of Americans placing moral scrutiny on their to-do list, we find there is little interest. Even though a majority of Americans consider people's morals and values to be errant, just one out of every twenty ranks this as the most pressing issue facing the nation today.[6] Perhaps the gap between understanding the need and adopting a sense of urgency and commitment for the task indicates that the hill of moral restoration seems too steep to climb.

In fact, given that the moral continuum indicates we are moving steadily toward moral anarchy, the most relevant question may be what it would take to reverse the trajectory. Such a change in direction would probably involve the following:

- Increased personal reading and study of the Bible, and accepting it as the sole and unchallenged moral standard for our society.
- A nationwide spiritual revival based on increased public exposure to effective biblical preaching and teaching about sin and morality, with personal accountability built in to the process.
- Cultural leaders committed to directing people toward lives characterized by traditional Judeo-Christian morality.
- Parents devoted to raising their children to adopt a biblical worldview and to disciplining them in ways that ingrain biblical morals.
- Public institutions, especially schools, accepting biblical morality as the standard for inclusion in educational materials as well as for behavioral standards on campus.

- Media that voluntarily and consistently produce content that conveys examples and messages consistent with biblical morals.
- Widespread acknowledgment of the painful and counterproductive consequences of behaving in ways that contradict scriptural principles.

17

POLITICAL
CORRECTNESS

Summary

The thought police have made a comeback.

Donald Trump, the trash-talking, egotistical presidential candidate who sought the Republican nomination in 2015–2016, made a big deal about his refusal to say things that were politically correct and claimed his candor in the face of the politically correct movement was one of the reasons for his appeal and a pragmatic demonstration of his leadership.

But Trump wasn't the only one who called out the movement. Even apolitical, mild-mannered people like legendary comedian Jerry Seinfeld—internationally known for his eponymous, long-running hit TV sitcom he described as "a show about nothing"—got in on the controversy. Seinfeld is renowned for his style of mild observational humor, but even he admitted to altering his career path because of the PC movement. Few people consider his comedy to be edgy, in the sense that a Chris Rock, Louis C.K., or Chelsea Handler might

131

push the envelope of decorum. But during an interview with ESPN's Colin Cowherd in June of 2015, Seinfeld admitted, "I don't play colleges, but I hear a lot of people tell me, 'Don't go near colleges, they're so PC.'" The comedian went on to scold college students, noting that they are prone to criticizing anyone who does not toe the liberal line. "'That's racist. That's sexist. That's prejudice.' They don't even know what they're talking about."

In another interview after his comments raised a liberal outcry, Seinfeld added, "There's a creepy PC thing out there that really bothers me."

Indeed, the PC police have been very active since the election of Barack Obama. The president actually signed a bill into law in 2012 that enables the government to prosecute anyone deemed guilty of critical words, political protest, or peaceful but troublesome assembly in an area where government officials happen to be present.[1]

Many activists have been equally as insistent on limiting the speech of those with whom they disagree. When the French satirists at *Charlie Hebdo* published cartoons about Muhammad and were consequently murdered by Islamic terrorists, a full-scale ideological war broke out between the right-wingers who supported the cartoonists' right to free speech and the left-wingers who accused the dead cartoonists of hate speech and racism. Leftist media such as the *New York Times* jumped into the fray by refusing to publish the cartoons that the terrorists considered blasphemy.

Political correctness has reared its head in other numerous ways. For instance, in recent years a growing number of college graduation speakers have been "disinvited" after the PC crowd raised vociferous objections to the political views of those speakers.

- Controversial talk show host Bill Maher was barred from giving the commencement speech at University of California, Berkeley after more than six thousand students signed a petition to block his appearance. The petition described Maher, who has been an equal opportunity offender on his show, as a "blatant bigot and racist."

- Smith College canceled an appearance by Christine Lagarde, managing director of the International Monetary Fund, because protesters claimed her organization was imperialist, oppressed women across the world, and relied on corrupt and patriarchal systems.

- Former secretary of state Condoleezza Rice declined an invitation to give a commencement address at Rutgers University after protesters claimed she violated human rights, gave authority to the CIA to engage in torture tactics, was responsible for the destruction of Iraq, and adhered to policies and actions that debased humanity. The protest was triggered by professors at the school and then carried on by students, causing Rice to bow out.

- Butler University rescinded an invitation to Supreme Court Chief Justice John Roberts because he was deemed "too controversial."

- Numerous other campuses revoked invitations because of the political views of those under consideration. Those potential speakers included Vice President Dick Cheney; former governor and presidential candidate Mitt Romney; former secretary of health and human services and governor Kathleen Sebelius; neurosurgeon Ben Carson (who later ran for president); former secretary of state, US senator, and presidential candidate Hillary Clinton; and conservative pundit Ann Coulter.

America's colleges have created an unhealthy educational environment. Professor Laura Kipnis, who teaches at Northwestern University, says, "The new codes sweeping American campuses aren't just a striking abridgment of everyone's freedom, they're also intellectually embarrassing. Sexual paranoia reigns; students are trauma cases waiting to happen. If you wanted to produce a pacified, cowering citizenry, this would be the method. And in that sense, we're all the victims." The campus environment has become, in the words of liberal columnist Michelle Goldberg, "intellectually stifling."[2]

Even liberal stalwarts, such as retired Harvard Law School professor Alan Dershowitz, have decried the closing of the minds of American college students. The erudite legal scholar said that "the fog of fascism is descending quickly over many American universities." Reacting to protests and other actions from students at Yale and the University of Missouri, he commented that "these are the same people who claim they are seeking diversity. The last thing many of these students want is real diversity, diversity of ideas. They may want superficial diversity, diversity of gender, diversity of color, but they don't want diversity of ideas. . . . It is the worst kind of hypocrisy. They want complete freedom over their sex lives, over their personal lives, over the use of drugs, but they want mommy and daddy, dean, and president to please give them a safe place, to protect them from ideas that maybe are insensitive. . . . You have to call these things what they are: double standards, hypocrisy, bigotry, McCarthyism."[3]

These toxic college environments have encouraged students to force their schools to pull the plug on businesses whose owners do not conform to liberal views. A prime example is the fast food chain Chick-fil-A. The chain's CEO, Dan Cathy, was crestfallen by the Supreme Court's decision in 2013 that it was unconstitutional not to recognize same-sex marriages. Cathy took to Twitter, tweeting, "Sad day for our nation; founding fathers would be ashamed of our gen. to abandon wisdom of the ages re: cornerstone of strong societies."[4]

In response, colleges, such as Johns Hopkins, Elon University, and Indiana University Bloomington, all voted to refrain from any future business dealings with Chick-fil-A. Based on Cathy's comments, the chain was cited for being sexually discriminatory and making "decisive statements" against homosexuals, creating what the *National Review* described as a "new spirit of intolerance" on our nation's campuses.[5]

The PC Movement had a banner year on college campuses in 2015. To facilitate appropriate behavior—or, as some would say, destroy free speech—some schools have sought to codify illegitimate speech. Wesleyan University made headlines by defunding its school newspaper in retaliation for a conservative op-ed piece written by one of its students who is an Iraq War veteran.[6] But leading the parade of schools gone wild is the University of Wisconsin–Milwaukee, which banned the use of the term "politically correct" because it implies that someone is too sensitive—and, of course, in this day and age you can never be too sensitive.[7] The school labeled the use of the term an act of "microaggression." Not to be left out, a fracas broke out at Duke University over the use of the term "man up." Yale students went nuts over culturally insensitive Halloween costumes, demanding that professors who were not incensed over such transgressions be terminated for their insensitivity to such insensitivity.[8]

The concept of being politically correct was introduced to American culture in the 1970s by political philosophers, feminists, radical-left college students, and journalists. In the early 1990s, however, conservative firebrand Dinesh D'Souza applied the term to characterize a body of left-wing perspectives that were aggressively promoted and vehemently defended by liberal apologists, academia, and the mainstream media. Their views typically related to public policies or statements concerning ethnicity, affirmative action, feminism, homosexuality, egalitarianism, class divisions, multiculturalism, military actions, religious beliefs, and the like.

Using the phrase was meant to call attention to language or ideas that liberals considered offensive to their ideology—and to note that conservatives considered such push back to be censorship, spiritually offensive, or indicators of liberals being overly sensitive.

Some have suggested that the ultimate goal of PC demands is to undermine conservative points of view, especially those based on Christian values and beliefs. While political correctness was initially promoted on college campuses across the nation, the advent of social media enabled PC thinking to gain a wider platform and audience, and injected a harsher, more combative tone to the tenor of online communications.

The unfortunate truth about the gathering strength of political correctness is that it compromises our freedom and depresses healthy conversation. When Americans are no longer free—or no longer *feel* free—to hold or express opinions that conflict with the perspectives promoted by certain vocal or activist sectors of society, we are headed down a dangerous path.

Key Facts

- 57 percent of adults believe America has become too politically correct. That includes 74 percent of adults who are registered Republicans and 66 percent who are Independent but only 35 percent of registered Democrats. Perhaps surprisingly, another one out of six—predominantly Democrats—says we are not PC enough.[9]

- The Pew Research Center discovered that among adults they characterize as "consistently liberal," close to half (44 percent) have hidden, blocked, defriended, or stopped following someone on Facebook because they disagreed with the political content of that person's postings. Less than one-third of those who are "consistently conservative" (31 percent) censored people in the same manner.[10]

- Just one-third of the public (33 percent) trusts the Supreme Court "a great deal" to properly handle and protect free speech in America.[11]

**Change in Views on Political Correctness
in the United States, 2010–2014**

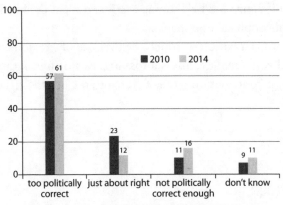

Sources: Rasmussen Reports; October 2010, N=1,000; June 2014, N=1,000.

Outlook and Interpretation

Neither liberals nor conservatives have cornered the market on hostility toward opposing political views, but the reemergence and growing intensity of political correctness is an unfortunate sign of the country's current divided nature. With Millennials widely engaged in the advance of the PC movement, nothing on the horizon suggests such ideological hostilities and behavioral totalitarianism will be ending.

Until we have political, educational, family, and religious leaders who model the willingness to respectfully entertain the ideas of their opponents and intelligently but calmly discuss conflicting ideas with the aim of improving the state of the world, the environment will become increasingly polluted by negativity and irrationality.

Christians, in particular, have a responsibility to lead the way in this area. Scripture exhorts us to engage in conversations that are "gracious and attractive so that you will have the right response for everyone" (Col. 4:6). We are called to interact with people using speech that is not "foul or abusive" but, rather, is "good and helpful, so that your words may be an encouragement to those who hear them" (Eph. 4:29). There does not appear to be any biblical reference to pleasing God by winning every argument or shutting down one's philosophical opponents.

America is a nation in which the practice of gracious conversation and congenial debate is a lost art. Restoring that art would be a major contribution by the Church to the health of the nation.

18

CONFIDENCE IN
INSTITUTIONS

Summary

Institutions are formal structures that stabilize patterns of behavior and facilitate social order and the central values that define and support a society. Changes within a culture are mediated by its social institutions and how they address problems and shape norms related to relationships, power, purpose, knowledge, and spirituality. People's confidence in the future and in their society is directly related to the degree of confidence they have in the social institutions that promote the culture's values, procedures, and public objectives.

The cultural reconfiguration that has been brewing in the United States, particularly over the past decade, has both been influenced by the nation's institutions and posed serious challenges to the identity and influence of those institutions. This has been an era of positive growth for a handful of them but a time of tumult and discomfort for many others.

Before the start of the new millennium, during the fast and furious 1990s, the cracks in the wall had already appeared for some of the more aggressive institutions. A decline in influence and clarity of message was evident for the likes of the news media, Congress, organized labor, big business, and the criminal justice system. The economic crisis during the first decade of the new millennium, along with scandals in the Catholic Church and the ideological conflict that introduced a new level of political gridlock, triggered a period of widespread public confusion and mistrust. America's central institutions have been slow to understand and effectively respond to people's insecurities and uncertainties, creating a consistently deepening lack of faith in the country's leaders and social system.

Of the fourteen major social institutions whose public standing has been tracked for several decades, 80 percent have experienced significant declines in public confidence. The steepest declines have been associated with banks (confidence in their performance has plummeted by 15 percentage points in the past twenty years), churches (also down 15 points), primary political institutions (Congress has lost 13 points on the confidence scale, while the US Supreme Court and the presidency have each dropped 12 points), and television news organizations have also declined by a dozen points. Other entities that have endured noteworthy declines include the public schools (−9 points), the police (−8 points), and newspapers, along with TV news, the other significant news source (−6 points).[1]

The crisis of confidence in foundational institutions is not simply that people have less confidence in such institutions but that few people in total believe these institutions will rise to the occasion and serve their needs well. Of the fourteen major institutions regularly evaluated, only two are currently inspiring sufficient confidence in the American people to be trusted to do what is right and to consistently advance the best interests of the public. Those two are the military (72 percent high confidence level) and the police (52 percent, but on the decline).[2]

In contrast, eleven of the fourteen institutions have generated high confidence among fewer than four out of ten Americans. Six of those are on a trajectory to take their confidence scores even lower than they are today. Five institutions—churches, banks, Congress, the presidency, and the police—have slipped in public confidence by more than 10 percentage points in the past decade alone.[3]

As precarious as the national condition is in relation to core institutions, recovery is still possible. Looking at the public's "net confidence scores" in relation to the fourteen entities, the good news is that half of them still retain generally positive impressions in the minds and hearts of the people. In other words, a larger contingency of people have a great deal or quite a lot of confidence in the institution than have little or no confidence in it. The difference between the scores at the two ends of the confidence continuum is positive. In several cases, the scores are so distinctly positive as to suggest that people's trust in those institutions is spurring confidence that other institutions will figure out how to more profitably navigate the rapids of cultural change.

Those hope-giving institutions are the military, the police, the medical system, and churches. Small businesses, which traditionally have not been tracked as a key social institution but have indisputably become one, also fare extremely well in public confidence.

Key Facts

Confidence in Social Institutions, 1995–2015

Social Institution	High Confidence			Change	Net Score
	2015	2005	1995	1995–2015	2015
Military	72%	74%	64%	+8 points	+65 points
Police	52	63	58	-6	+34
Churches/organized religion	42	53	57	-15	+19
Medical system	37	42	41	-4	+12
Presidency	33	44	45	-12	-7
US Supreme Court	32	41	44	-12	+7
Public schools	31	37	40	-9	+3
Banks	28	49	43	-15	+2
Newspapers	24	28	30	-6	-10

continued

Social Institution	High Confidence			Change	Net Score
	2015	2005	1995	1995–2015	2015
Organized labor/unions	24	24	26	-2	-7
Criminal justice system	23	26	20	+3	-11
Television news	21	28	33	-12	-20
Big business	21	22	21	0	-16
Congress	8	11	22	-14	-45

High confidence: percent who say "a great deal" or "quite a lot" of confidence.

Change 1995–2015: difference between high confidence scores of 1995 and 2015.

Net score: difference between high confidence score and low confidence score (based on the percentage who say "a little" or "no" confidence).

Source: Gallup Organization, http://www.gallup.com/poll/1597/Confidence-Institutions.aspx.

Net Change in Americans with "A Great Deal of Confidence" in Selected Social Institutions, 1995–2015

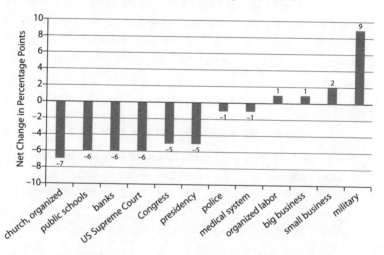

Source: Gallup Organization, Confidence in Institutions, http://www.gallup.com/poll/1597/Confidence -Institutions.aspx.

Outlook and Interpretation

Competing forces are at work here. On the one hand, the American people are rather forgiving and resilient in their attitudes toward people and institutions. Bill Clinton and George W. Bush, for vastly different reasons, both experienced a nosedive and then a gradual revival of public confidence. On the institutional front, we can already see banks are making a slow return to the public's good graces after people's confidence was shaken by multiple banking incidents a decade ago.

On the other hand, once people write off an entity, it takes a lot of time and intentional effort for the entity to regain public trust. People demand proof of change beyond a simple public relations campaign. Just ask Michael Phelps, Tiger Woods, Dan Rather, or Lance Armstrong.

The same principle is at play with institutions. Congress is filled with well-intentioned, intelligent, industrious individuals, but as an institution it has yet to convince the American people that it is moving in the right direction for the right reasons. The presidency has lost its shine under the last two presidents, and it will take several terms of stellar behavior and performance by new holders of that office before higher levels of confidence in the office are restored. Big business is in a precarious position regarding public confidence, given continual reports of malfeasance and profiteering by high-profile corporations and their executives—especially during a period of overall economic stagnation. The news media, amid a flurry of studies showing consistent bias in news reporting, has abused the public trust so routinely that it will take a prolonged period of overt fairness in reporting to repair the reputational damage.

Some institutions, such as churches, will struggle to reach the lofty heights of public confidence they experienced prior to this past decade. Millions of young adults are jettisoning organized religion from their lives and questioning the theological underpinnings of the major faith groups. Add to that the media's gleeful reporting of the Catholic Church's sex scandals or the seemingly regular incidents of Protestant church leaders abusing congregational funds, and convincing the public that churches add more value to society than they extract will be an uphill battle.

Churches, of course, add tremendous value to society. They address the spiritual and emotional needs of tens of millions of people on an ongoing basis. But beyond that, America's churches provide food, clothing, and shelter to the homeless and disadvantaged; serve the needs of senior citizens; host public forums to inform people about various public issues; provide child- and health-care services; offer alternatives to public schools; establish connections and community among people; provide counseling services; and so much more. Many, if not most, of the public services churches provide are offered at no or below-market cost. Adequately communicating to the public their provision of those benefits, without losing their altruistic motivations and humility, is the challenge for religious institutions.

How has the United States stayed united during such a time of distrust and disappointment? Partially, people have moderated their expectations, lowering their standards to accept a lesser level of institutional performance—which, in turn, has caused millions to become more cynical and selfish. A culture can endure that response for a brief moment in history, but a prolonged negative attitude toward central institutions typically produces unhealthy shifts in the society. This next decade will be pivotal for renewing people's faith in core institutions, which will release new levels of enthusiasm and energy in regard to restoring America's cultural foundations.

One irony of the situation is that a significant degree of people's confidence in our institutions is determined by a pair of institutions that have low and declining levels of confidence. Television news and newspapers generate a high level of confidence among fewer than one out of every four Americans, yet we develop a meaningful share of our perceptions about the other institutions based on the portrait painted for us by these relatively untrustworthy organizations. Perhaps the advance of new technologies will provide a sufficiently reconstructed field of information options—through social media, mobile apps, and other means—to compensate for what the mainstream media typically provides, and then our confidence levels in trustworthy institutions will once again rise.

19
RETIREMENT

Summary

Many Americans think of retirement as their "golden years"—the reward at the end of several decades of work when they can finally relax and enjoy life to a greater degree than was possible when an occupation consumed most of their waking hours. Almost two-thirds of us who are not retired (63 percent) look forward to those years when working is a choice rather than an expectation and financial necessity.[1]

The aging Baby Boom population, the numerically huge generation that has redefined every avenue of life it has encountered, is making retirement a hot topic. That is particularly true in relation to the impact of Boomer retirement on the nation's economy and lifestyle patterns. Since the day Boomers began turning sixty-five (January 1, 2011) through the end of 2029 (when the last Boomer will reach that age), an average of ten thousand Boomers per day will reach their sixty-fifth birthday. By 2030, people sixty-five or older will constitute one out of every five individuals in the nation—up from one out of eight as recently as 2010. In 2015, 48 million people were sixty-five

146

or older; that number will skyrocket to 74 million in 2030, which constitutes a 54 percent increase in just fifteen years. (And keep in mind that millions of people retire, voluntarily or involuntarily, prior to reaching their sixty-fifth birthday.)[2]

But several realities are causing the average worker in America to have to wait longer than expected or hoped for before they can escape from the workplace. Chief among those realities are the changes that have been redefining the national economy and will affect retirees—increased cost of living, lack of increase in the average household's income in more than a decade, depressed levels of savings, decimated pensions, and threat of a bankrupt Social Security system in the near future. Add to that the fact that people are living longer lives—necessitating more savings than ever before—and you can understand how preparing for retirement is more challenging than it has been in at least a half-century.

How much longer will workers have to wait before they can slip into the retirement phase of their lives? In 1991, the average age of retirement was sixty-two for men and fifty-nine for women; it has since risen to sixty-four for men and sixty-two for women and is projected to continue slowly rising over the next few years.[3]

Surprisingly, people's retirement plans bear a limited relationship to their retirement behavior. Although most people plan to retire at sixty-five or older, half of all retirees leave the workforce before they had planned to, usually due to health issues (either their own or those of someone for whom they must provide primary care), the downsizing or closure of their workplace, or changes in skills required by the job.[4]

Most people closing in on retirement (63 percent) admit they expect to keep working, albeit not necessarily in the same industry or profession. About four out of ten adults (38 percent) say they will do little or no paid work during their retirement. The rest are about evenly divided between those who say they will do some work, most likely in their current line of activity or industry (34 percent), and those who plan to work but in a different line of activity (29 percent). Among those who plan to keep working, three out of four attribute that activity to their desire to keep working, while the rest expect to work out of financial need. The research also shows that those who have the lowest levels of education and income are the least likely to plan to continue working.[5]

Among those who look forward to retiring, the pursuits that appeal the most are spending time with family, relaxing, volunteering, doing work they enjoy, and traveling. Unexpectedly, the research shows that the top priorities among all of those pursuits are volunteering and working.[6]

However, if economists are correct, many people close to retirement may find that either their retirement date is unexpectedly delayed or they are not able to live as comfortably as they had planned. For instance, among those who plan to retire at the earliest age at which one can begin to draw Social Security benefits, only 30 percent of those households are financially prepared for retirement. Among those who expect to call it quits when they reach the current full retirement age (sixty-six and rising to sixty-seven as of 2026), barely half (55 percent) are financially ready for the transition. By age seventy, however, a large majority (86 percent) are prepared to take the plunge.[7]

Studies that examine people's preparedness for retirement vary substantially on the prognosis, but almost all of them agree that millions of households have done too little to get ready for the financial realities of retirement. The median nest egg, including Social Security benefits, among people fifty-five to sixty-four years of age—i.e., the group that has had the longest time to save and is the closest to pulling the trigger on retirement—is likely to provide an average monthly income of less than $1,600 over the duration of their post-work life.[8] And as modest as that sum is, its purchasing power could be significantly diminished over time due to inflation.

Millions of these older Americans may be forced to continue working in order to live in reasonable comfort. Baby Boomers, for instance, hope to retire with an annual income from various sources—Social Security, pension plans, IRAs, 401(k)s, and savings—of about $45,000. Indications are that the typical Boomer has not put away enough to receive even half of that amount. Many of them will likely have to continue in the labor force, even if only part time. The US Bureau of Labor Statistics notes that one out of five people sixty-five or older—a proportion that can be expected to rise—is currently in the labor force.[9]

In fact, the Federal Reserve Board estimates that the gap between how much money people are saving for retirement and what they will need to live at their current standard of living is $7.7 trillion. Part of that gap is due to the fact that so many soon-to-be-retirees (more than three out of five households) still owe money on their home, credit cards, and other debts.[10]

One topic raised in conversations among older people is the possibility of moving to a different location, often one that features better weather or superior senior services. The facts tell a different story though. In recent years, people sixty-five and older have been the least likely to relocate—only 3 percent moved, compared to 14 percent of the rest of the population. In fact, more than three-quarters of the elders who did move stayed within the same state.[11]

Key Facts

- The median age of retirement today is sixty-four for men and sixty-two for women.[12]
- Just 9 percent of current workers plan to retire before age sixty, but 36 percent of current retirees wound up leaving the workplace before reaching sixty.[13]
- Largely due to financial constraints, the percentage of people who plan to retire at or after age sixty-five has risen from 11 percent in 1991 to 36 percent today.[14]

- The most common reasons for retiring before desired include health issues (in 60 percent of early retirements), downsizing or closures of their workplace (27 percent), or changes in skills required by the job (10 percent).[15]
- 48 million people were sixty-five or older in the United States in 2015. The Census Bureau estimates that there will be 74 million adults sixty-five or older in 2030. During that fifteen-year period, the total US population is expected to increase by 12 percent; the sixty-five-plus portion of the population will increase by 54 percent.[16]
- The Federal Reserve Board estimates that for people who will retire to maintain their current standard of living, there is a $7.7 trillion income gap.[17]
- The average retiree is estimated to spend $245,000 on health-care costs over the duration of their retirement years.[18]

65-Plus Population in the United States

(in millions of people)

Year	Population
1990	33.2
2000	35
2010	40.3
2020	56
2030	72.8
2040	79.7
2050	83.7

Source: Census Bureau estimates, www.census.gov.

Outlook and Interpretation

Admittedly, being a Boomer renders me less sensitive to the strangeness of living in a society in which every fifth person is my age or older. However, recalling what it was like when I was a teenager or young adult visiting Miami or Phoenix during the winter, I can imagine that Busters and Millennials struggle with the seeming plague of elderly that has surrounded them. As someone who is part of the "Boomer-in-the-python" problem, I don't really feel their pain, but I can certainly understand it and sympathize with their plight.

The unchecked impact of a growing retirement class is already troubling the minds of many. One recent survey discovered that nearly half of the nation (47 percent) is feeling pessimistic about the coming impact of a massive wave of retiring Boomers.[19] Is it possible that such pessimism could result in an even deeper generational divide? Can we expect future political leaders to have to address strident demands for government reductions in services and benefits doled out to the elderly, a tact that has been considered beyond political expediency to date?

The implications of Boomers having to remain in the workforce beyond the "normal" retirement age are huge. As the United States struggles to reinvigorate a national economy that has been sluggish, at best, for more than a decade, millions of Americans are discouraged by stagnant wages, dead-end jobs, or radical cuts in benefits. Millions of others remain unemployed or underemployed, with a growing segment not even counted in those figures because they have given up hope of finding a job. Add to that millions of elderly Boomers who must remain working to maintain a reasonable standard of living and not default on mortgages, loans, and other financial obligations, while handling the rising cost of their expanding medical and health-care needs, and the resulting picture is not pretty. It is also possible, if not likely, that many of those older workers will become less productive as time goes on, and legitimate questions linger about what kind of attitude they will have toward work during the years they had hoped to be relaxing and enjoying the good life.

However, many employers admit that they appreciate the typical Boomer's strong work ethic and sense of responsibility, especially when compared to the too-often lackadaisical performance of younger workers. If there were a way of empowering Boomers to motivate and mentor younger employees, perhaps a productive win-win outcome would be realized.

One of the most uplifting findings in relation to retirement is that Millennials seem to understand the importance of saving money for their post-work years. Studies have indicated that while the typical Boomer began saving for retirement at thirty-five, Millennials typically start their long-term savings effort at twenty-two. If they can be encouraged to protect and increase the pace of their retirement savings over the long haul, the retirement income gap could be mitigated.

20
THE FUTURE

Summary

The complexities of modern life take a toll on Americans. Not only are they overwhelmed by the volume and breadth of information about what's going on in the world and what they face individually, but also they are increasingly worried about numerous possibilities that could undermine the quality of life in America. While Americans generally remain guardedly optimistic about their personal future, they tend to be less sanguine about the future of the nation and other people—and especially about the future that our children and grandchildren will inherit.

Today's level of optimism is well below the levels recorded in the recent past. For several decades Americans believed the nation was headed to a better tomorrow. That thinking, however, seems to have run its course—at least temporarily. Soon after the terrorist attacks on September 11, 2001, Americans began to see things differently. The prolonged recession that started in 2007 fueled continued concern about the future. It's now an era of domestic and global challenges, and most people are entering this new age with their eyes open and expectations dampened.

One of the casualties along the way has been the American Dream. The Dream held that anyone willing to work hard, make strategic sacrifices, and use their cumulative resources wisely could get ahead in life. It included pursuing a college education, finding a challenging and rewarding job, getting married and raising children in a positive and safe environment, and enjoying a secure and comfortable life in a free country. The key to facilitating that dream was the willingness to balance freedom and responsibility.

Today, however, a sizeable majority of citizens believe a large share of present-day adults and a majority of future Americans will not be able to experience that dream. Most Americans contend that the obstacles to achieving the Dream are bigger than ever, things are not likely to get better in the foreseeable future, and even those who are willing to do what it takes to get ahead will not have the opportunity to do so.

However, the data contain one striking anomaly: most people remain optimistic about their own future. Almost nine out of ten describe themselves as optimistic about their future, a point of view based on multiple factors. For instance, about seven out of ten contend they are now, or will soon be, living the American Dream. Seven out of ten admit to being happy in their employment, and two out of three claim to be relatively stable and secure financially.[1] These figures are a reflection of an American hallmark: an unrealistic and indefensibly positive perception of one's own character, intelligence, capabilities, and future prospects. We may not believe in the country's future, but we continue to embrace an upbeat personal narrative about who we are and where we are headed, regardless of the state of the nation.

At the same time that we embrace a Pollyannaish view of ourselves, large majorities proclaim that the country is headed in the wrong direction, the economy is in trouble, society is losing its way morally and spiritually, global tensions are serious and likely to escalate, government is neither competent nor trustworthy, and children are getting the short end of the stick.

In fact, adults are twice as likely to believe that most children will grow up to be worse off than those youngsters' parents as they are to say they will be better off in the future. Furthermore, compared to a decade ago, only half as many adults now believe the current generation of children will have a better life than their parents experienced.

What stands in the way of fulfilling people's dreams and maximizing their future? Given the complexities of modern life, the list of worries and fears that trouble Americans is daunting but not surprising. The most widespread concerns are government corruption, not having enough money to live, contracting a serious illness, growing old, pollution or toxic waste contamination of soil and water, having financial data hacked on the internet, and full implementation of the Affordable Care Act (aka Obamacare). Between one-quarter and one-half of all adults admit they are very worried or concerned about one or more of these possibilities.[2]

True to their renowned entrepreneurial form, though, most Americans face their demons head-on and reinvent themselves. About half of all adults indicate they have already confronted and overcome serious life challenges by undertaking a life makeover, and another one-fifth of the nation plans to do so. Such personal transformations are most common in the areas of health and wellness, coping with a shift in life stage, altering existing attitudes, and realigning one's typical experiences and types of involvement.[3] Given the alternatives, most people seem willing to attempt a personal redesign to improve their life. Without such a can-do mind-set, our nation's pessimism levels would certainly be higher.

Key Facts

- 86 percent of Americans are optimistic about their own future.[4]
- 69 percent describe the obstacles to experiencing the American Dream as more extreme than ever.[5]

- Six out of ten (59 percent) say the American Dream has become impossible for most Americans to achieve.[6]
- 54 percent say America is no longer a place where everyone has the opportunity to get ahead and move up to a better standard of living.[7]
- 21 percent believe today's children will have a better life than their parents experienced. In 2001, 49 percent held that view.[8]
- Almost twice as many adults believe most children will grow up to be worse off than their parents (63 percent) as believe they will be better off (34 percent).[9]
- 55 percent of adults say they have coped with past challenges by "reinventing" themselves. Another 21 percent say they expect to do so in the near term.[10]

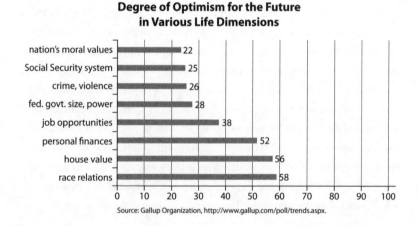

Degree of Optimism for the Future in Various Life Dimensions

Source: Gallup Organization, http://www.gallup.com/poll/trends.aspx.

Outlook and Interpretation

The more comfortable Americans become with the countless technological innovations that define their daily experiences, the less likely they are to ever see a simpler lifestyle return. Along with the

156

reduction of that possibility comes the potential for a decrease in fears, anxieties, worries, and concerns about life.

Perhaps the most disturbing shift is the loss of the traditional American Dream. A new ideal has emerged—one we might call the New Millennium Dream. This portrait of a preferable tomorrow features a wholly different perspective on freedom and responsibility. In short, the New Dream is driven by individuals' demands for freedom and rights they feel entitled to; the application of a personalized moral code based on situational truth; a willingness to work only as hard as may be required to get by; and a dogged pursuit of happiness in the guise of comfort, convenience, choices, connections, and experiences.[11]

While it may be the new ideal, it is not a recipe for the restoration of a strong and vibrant America.

Meanwhile, the nation's children today face a uniquely demanding future—and one that is not likely to be as fulfilling or robust as the one their elders had expected to experience when they were kids. The many challenges confronting the nation—in education, governance, public health, economics, national security, and more—will cause them more tensions and pressures than their predecessors faced.

Adults and children alike will continue to combat a growing and ever-changing list of worries and fears. The introduction of new and more sophisticated technologies is likely to alter people's lifestyles and the risks associated with those lifestyles. Some of the existing fears besetting Americans, like increased government corruption, environmental disasters, and being victims of hacking, are likely to come to pass. How Americans respond to these hardships will greatly influence their feelings about the future.

Will optimism make a comeback anytime soon? It is likely to be at least one more cultural cycle—and maybe more—before a majority of Americans can realistically adopt an upbeat and hopeful mind-set.

157

PART 4

STANDING AT THE CROSSROADS

21
WHAT YOU
CAN DO

This is a desperate time for America. Whether you want to admit it or not, it is difficult to be a follower of Jesus Christ, read the preceding chapters, and draw any conclusion other than that. No matter what topic you choose to examine, the deeper your evaluation goes, the more certain you can be that the nation is in trouble and moving in the wrong direction.

Below is a summary of the data discussed in this book in simple and direct form:

- The morals of Americans are more representative of Sodom and Gomorrah than the kingdom of God.
- People's religious beliefs have only a tangential and diminishing relationship to the teachings of the Bible.
- Trust and confidence in the institutions designed to foster appropriate living, from churches to the government, are justifiably plummeting.
- The political system has turned chaotic and unproductive, and most Americans no longer believe that system serves them well—or is committed to trying.

- People's lifestyles are characterized by behavior and goals that are the opposite of that which pleases and reflects the image of God; humans are largely selfish, pleasure-seeking, lust-filled, jealous, quarrelsome, greedy, dishonest, and unfaithful creatures. Perhaps humankind has always fit that profile, but those who diligently seek God's righteousness recognize such deficiencies and pursue His forgiveness and restoration without ceasing—a quest that does not characterize America today.
- A majority of the country's churches seem to have lost sight of their God-given purpose and have proven to be ineffective at leading people back to the righteous path.

As Jesus said, "The gateway to life is very narrow and the road is difficult, and only a few ever find it" (Matt. 7:14).

It is beyond dispute that America's condition today bears little resemblance to that of a nation that honors God and reflects His values, principles, vision, and purposes. We are like an airplane that lifted off the runway two degrees off its flight plan and refused to make the necessary course corrections, resulting in the aircraft landing hundreds of miles from its intended destination. That's bad enough, but the most unfortunate part of the journey is that after landing so far off the mark, the pilots and passengers alike contend that it is precisely where they had hoped to land and those who say otherwise do not know what they are talking about. That's a case of world-class denial.

This is not a pretty or uplifting picture. For those of us who aspire to be Christlike, it is outright embarrassing and heartbreaking.

A Christ follower believes God gave us the Bible for something more than pleasure reading. It is His words of guidance for our lifestyle, as well as His portrait of social order and cultural sensibility. He is gracious enough to allow us to work out the details of how to construct a society that reflects His principles and obeys His commands, but He is unequivocal about the identity of a godly society's foundational qualities, such as truth, love, compassion, mercy, humility, and so forth.

As we consider those qualities, we must then examine the society we have created to ascertain whether we are incorporating His principles and obeying His commands. If someone who knew nothing about Christ or the Bible were plopped into American society today and told this nation is a reflection of the principles of God, what portrait would they paint of that God? Would their sense of our culture capture the heartbeat of the Creator? Would that visitor receive a faithful glimpse of the nature, purposes, and principles of God from the society we have developed?

This closing portion of the book is intended to be a subjective statement about a few crucial elements required to restore the heart and soul of America. As we consider what it will take to turn around our nation, I am not arguing that electing the right people, changing certain laws, altering media content and exposure, or redirecting what is taught in our schools will fix all the problems. Those actions are certainly necessary, but in so doing we would merely address the symptoms of a far larger and deeper problem that must be attacked. That problem is a people problem, not a systemic problem. America would be in trouble no matter what system of government, form of church practice, or economic standard we embraced. To fix our problem we must address our people issue.

Simply put, we have not committed ourselves to the purpose He has for each of us (vision), we are not willing to pay the price of becoming who He made and calls us to be (transformation), and we do not behave like Jesus because we do not think like Him (worldview). Let's take a brief look at each of these challenges.

Shared Vision

The Bible teaches that if we do not have God's vision, we will waste our time and energy, noting that "when people do not accept divine guidance, they run wild" (Prov. 29:18). That's what God's vision is: divine guidance designed to give us the tracks to run on. When we pursue our own vision rather than God's, we operate without the benefit of His perfect wisdom and direction and full blessing, relying instead on our distorted perspectives and motivations.

The Church is meant to be the accumulation of people who take their cues from God, seeking to bring His vision into reality. This implies that each person contributes some morsel of value to the aggregate outcome that His vision leads to. But this also means we must embrace a shared vision—a mental portrait of the preferable future He has designed for us.[1] The combination of skills, talents, spiritual gifts, life experiences, information, insights, relationships, tangible resources, and opportunities that He has allowed us to have provide the basis for our capacity to pursue His vision with enthusiasm. If I carry out my role and responsibilities, you complete yours, and the other authentic followers of Jesus fulfill theirs, then the end result will be a spectacular, redeemed future. Only when we pursue our own dreams and desires do things get off track—as is readily evident in America today.

Have you taken the time and made the effort to grasp God's vision for your life? The heart of that vision will be how you bless God through the application of the resources He has entrusted to you for your time and God-determined purpose on this earth. Thus, one aspect of your gift to God is how you will bless the society in which you live. Always remember that neither your life nor His vision for your life is ultimately about you; it is about how you can express love to Him and other people.

God delivers His vision to you through various ways: prayer, Spirit-driven meditation, the Scriptures, teaching and preaching received, conversations with other believers, and even circumstances. You must specifically seek an understanding of God's unique plan for your life. His vision will blow you away. It is challenging and perhaps even scary because of the scope of the assignment given to you and the hardships involved. But He entreats you to "trust in the LORD with all your heart; do not depend on your own understanding. Seek His will in all you do, and He will show you which path to take" (Prov. 3:5–6). The vision He reveals to you will be beyond your human capabilities, but He is not relying solely on your personal capacity. You are operating as part of His team and, thus, have access to all the supernatural resources He will bring to your circumstances.

Knowing and pursuing God's vision for your life is both a divine assignment and a privilege. You cannot go wrong by committing your life to fulfilling that vision. And the culture in which you live will be enriched and shaped by that commitment to godly action. Imagine what would happen to the United States if all the people who are truly devoted to knowing, loving, and serving God—my research indicates that segment is more than seven million strong—were to consistently live like Jesus.

A few years ago I was reading a biography about Francis of Assisi, a profoundly spiritual man who was certainly devoted to knowing, loving, and serving God. The book included a phrase used to describe the context of Francis's times: "Men everywhere had but one desire—to devote themselves to some great and holy cause."[2] Wow! That's precisely what we're talking about: gaining a sense of purpose in life from devoting our remaining time to a God-ordained great and holy cause (i.e., God's vision for our life).

Based on the research I have carried out regarding the number of Americans who have been broken and have completely surrendered their lives to Christ, we may assume there are 12 million fully devoted followers of Christ amid this nation of 245 million adults. Do those 12 million constitute just a few grains of sand on the beach, virtually invisible among the great masses that are deaf to the voice of God? Or do they represent the holy remnant that God will use to restore this wayward nation? Can you envision the difference that 12 million people devoted to a great and holy cause could make? Do you want to be part of it and find out?

To which group do you belong—the masses eagerly and meaninglessly pursuing their own dreams or the 12 million making a difference through their devotion to a great and holy cause?

Transformation[3]

The process of allowing God to transform you into the person He envisioned you becoming is a lifelong challenge. Often, we believe we have dealt with our sin issue by asking Jesus to be our Savior, and after making that decision we move on to face the other challenges of life. We feel comforted in believing our place in Heaven is secure and we no longer have to fret about Satan's impact on our eternal life.

Unfortunately, there is a lot of misunderstanding and unfinished business related to our salvation. (And, yes, this topic is fraught with theological land mines, so I will attempt to tread carefully.) My research suggests that millions of Americans "say the prayer" that they assume guarantees them eternal salvation. But the research also confirms that a large share of those people do not develop a real "relationship" with Christ, they have not really broken rank with sin, and they are not truly living for God's purposes. Millions of people who have said a salvation prayer missed the primary caveat of that offer: one must be broken of sin, self, and society to truly be freed from the control of those influences and to become a follower of Christ.

The data indicate that very few people—currently about 5 percent of America's adults—have been broken by their understanding of and distaste for their offenses against God.[4] And shockingly, a huge majority of people who call themselves Christian—and even a majority of those who have specifically asked Jesus Christ to save them from their sins—believe a person can be saved without experiencing such brokenness.[5]

Unfortunately, they are wrong. Salvation doesn't exist without brokenness; anything less is a distortion of God's offer of wholeness and a reflection of the "cheap grace" Dietrich Bonhoeffer famously described. Genuine transformation cannot occur without the experience and acceptance of brokenness.

My six-year study on how God transforms lives and what difference such transformation makes to the individual and the world they influence indicates that the absence of brokenness is the missing link between faith and impact. Because so few Christians have pursued brokenness, the Church is not able to be the true Church Christ died for. If Christ's followers were to allow God to fully break them of sin, self, and society, the character and subsequent influence of His Church would be radically different than what we see in the Church and in the world today.

The Bible leaves no doubt as to the necessity of brokenness. Consider some of the evidence:

- King David lived life to the fullest—sometimes too full. In addition to other sins, he suffered from lust, engaged in adultery, and committed murder. To grab David's attention and teach him the seriousness of what he had willfully done, God allowed David's marriage to dissolve, his baby to die, and his older children to rebel against him. David was a man after God's heart, but God had to break him (2 Sam. 11–15).
- The apostle Paul was a brilliant scholar and skilled debater. But he was ruled by hatred (of Christians) and pride. God loved Paul enough to break him through blindness, beatings, imprisonment, mistrust, questions about his standing as an apostle, and public humiliation (Acts 9; 2 Cor. 6; 12).
- Jonah was a reluctant and disobedient prophet. He heard and refused God's call, preferring to let his enemies experience God's harsh judgment. Jonah's self-centeredness and lack of compassion for fellow sinners resulted in a life marked by emotional turmoil, physical peril, and public rejection (Jon. 1–4).
- Moses was a highly educated orphan, raised in a privileged environment and prepared for leadership. But after breaking away

from his Egyptian setting, he returned to lead God's people. Unfortunately, in one particular circumstance, he disobeyed God and beat a rock with a stick, ostensibly taking credit for a miracle God performed by generating water from that stone. That act of defiance displayed the level of pride and anger residing within Moses. In response, God allowed Israel's leader to complete the work of leading the Jews to the brink of the Promised Land but banned him from entering it (Num. 20).

Note that in each case God responded by more than simply doling out a punishment. He intended to break the heart of the sinner in order to reform their relationship with Him.

Moses's situation is especially instructive. To the untrained heart, it may seem as if Moses got a raw deal. Sure, he hit a rock with a stick because he was tired of God's people whining. That hardly seems worthy of depriving him the joy of experiencing the place God had reserved for Israel. He, after all, was a diligent leader who, based on little more than pure faith, had put up with doubters and complainers for years while miserably trekking through a desert. What would motivate God to react so sternly to such a minor miscue? To my human mind, the punishment did not fit the crime; it seemed way over the top. From my arrogant, self-absorbed perspective, it seemed blatantly unfair.

But that punishment was simply a necessary means to a glorious end. God's in-your-face response finally pierced Moses's spirit and enabled him to receive an incredible gift: brokenness. Through the ensuing brokenness, Moses was able to know God more genuinely, deeply, and completely. He was able to walk more closely with Him and serve Him more appropriately. He transitioned from self-centered leadership to God-centered service. And he was able to accept the loss of a prized earthly reward in exchange for an invaluable eternal reward.

Also, let's not overlook that Jesus Himself was broken. He had to experience such devastation, not because of anything He did but because of your sin and my sin. Even the holy Son of God was not spared the pain and suffering inherent in being separated from God because of our offensive choices. That our holy and righteous Savior was broken is the ultimate sign to us, God's offenders, of just how important it is to abandon anything that impedes our complete reliance on God for true life.

God broke almost every great biblical hero through multiple life crises or harsh circumstances designed for that purpose. Even the best of us need to be broken, fully and completely detached from our dalliance with sin, self, and society.

If you examine the individuals involved in all these instances, you'll see that God does not force us to accept brokenness. He always allows us to choose. But if you are wise, you will discover that you either allow God to use circumstances to wake and break you, or you may count on continuing to fight Him and suffering because of it.

Most people never realize that brokenness is actually a gift from God that demonstrates His awesome and unyielding love. We typically examine the circumstances He designed to guide us from a casual acquaintance to an intense and intimate lover of God and foolishly conclude that they are harmful to our well-being. In reality, they are God's means of bringing us to our knees before Him, in full-on repentance, enabling us to see the truth of who we are, who He is, how we treat Him, and how compassionate He is.

In our culture-aided confusion, we focus on the frustration, deprivation, sacrifice, pain, suffering, hardship, and persecution that God injects into our experience. We mistakenly assume that once we believe nice things about God and invest a few personal resources in the development of our faith, the appropriate response by our Father should be affirmation, comfort, pleasure, rewards, and happiness.

But that's only because we do not understand the nature of God, the magnitude of societal and personal depravity, the beauty of brokenness, or the pathway to genuine love.

If you are serious about honoring and loving God, eliminating your gnawing sense of spiritual discontent or incompleteness, and living your life to the fullest degree, then you have no choice but to embrace brokenness and to trust God alone to bring you through it.

An honest look at the Christian Church in America—and it may be true of believers around the world too—reveals that most Christians acknowledge the importance of brokenness but do everything they can to avoid experiencing it. Individual believers seek to avoid brokenness because American culture proclaims that it is for weak people—losers who don't have the strength, the smarts, the resources, or the resilience necessary to succeed in a competitive world. That same society also tempts people into believing that they don't need to be broken because the world enables them to have it all—if they set their sights on winning, play their cards right, and persevere.

An overwhelming majority of Americans have spent little or no time thinking about or preparing for brokenness. It is not something parents discuss with their children. It is not a lesson taught in schools, even Christian schools. It is not an outcome supported by government programs or rhetoric. In fact, brokenness is not likely to gain much attention from families, schools, or government because it requires a long-term view of life, truth, and purpose that places God and His ways at the center of the discussion. Instead, we conceive and promote strategies designed to help us live "in the moment" more effectively, ignoring the well-known truth that such a lifestyle is destined to fail. When comfortable survival and immediate gratification are a person's chief ends, their life is resigned to insignificance.

Churches are partly at fault for Christians not taking brokenness seriously. Because the perceived success of most churches is so intimately tied to the number of people attending, and because it is virtually impossible to draw (and retain) a crowd when the teaching promises the inevitable struggles that accompany brokenness, this topic gets little attention and is treated with little urgency. My studies have found that churchgoers are taught very little, if anything, about the beauty and necessity of being broken in order to pursue and experience wholeness. Few are allowed to reach the precipice of brokenness within their congregational context because individual happiness is more often accepted as a natural outcome and a higher end of the Christian life than the necessity of being crushed by one's offenses against God. Some churches even preach a theology that claims God will protect His people from all hurt and hardship.

My research about the transformational journey that God allows us to experience indicates that the pain and distress of being broken is necessary to facilitate personal and corporate wholeness. What makes brokenness so significant?

1. We are called to imitate the life of Christ.

One of the most pressing challenges followers of Christ face is mimicking what He modeled for us (Eph. 5:1). Christ assumed the burden of our sins, sins He did not commit, and was crushed by them. He did not savor that pain, but He embraced the brokenness that led not only to God's grace and Christ's own glorification but also to the justification and sanctification of hundreds of millions of human beings.

Many Christians in America talk about following Christ, but the true way to imitate Him is to eliminate the grip of sin, self, and society on our minds, hearts, and souls. That starts with seeing sin, self, and society for what they are—especially in contrast to the incomparable riches available through Jesus Christ—and then choosing to embrace the path of brokenness, surrender, submission, sacrifice, and service. Our salvation is not of our own making, but our sanctification is certainly related to our willingness to replicate the model that Jesus gave us: rejecting sin, allowing its weight to break us, and permitting God to restore us through our voluntary and comprehensive determination to live through Him and for Him.

2. Our intimacy with God is blocked by our love of other things and can only be restored by willingly becoming a broken vessel.

The concept of "fatal attraction" has no better application than in regard to things that get in the way of our relationship with God. Our lives are meant to be lived for Him and His purposes. Objectively, it doesn't get better than that. Yet, 99 percent of American adults—literally—have chosen to pursue beings, possessions, and conditions that relegate God to a secondary (or worse) position in our minds, hearts, and lives. Those preferences amount to our continuing affair with sin, self, and society.

In essence, we are adulterers until we voluntarily abandon those errant passions. If we do not master those distractions and preferences, they control us and keep us from being who God created us to be: His loving and obedient servants.

In our "sophisticated" culture, we denigrate any decision portrayed in black or white terms. In reality, our lives are based on a series of pivotal black or white decisions. The most important of those is: Will I or won't I live my life solely for the pleasure and benefit of God? Every subsequent choice in life is built on the foundation of that answer.

3. Brokenness precedes wholeness.

A friend challenged my thinking on this, noting that something must be whole before it can be broken. What he overlooked was that God conceived us to be holy before we chose to offend and replace Him in our lives, and that is what created the weakness in us that allows for the benefit of true brokenness. But, of course, once we have been separated from that which made us weak, we then have the opportunity to again be made strong by the One who has the strength to do all things.

Unless we understand and embrace our own brokenness, we are insulated from so many of God's glorious and desirable promises. Rejecting brokenness prevents us from:

- Experiencing all the promises God has made to us in His Word (2 Cor. 6:14–7:1; Heb. 6:9–12; 11:4–19; 2 Pet. 1:3–11).

- Becoming the "new creation" God envisions us to be (Rom. 12:2; 2 Cor. 5:17; Gal. 6:15; Eph. 4:24).

- Experiencing true freedom from the bondage of sin, self, and society (Rom. 6:14; Gal. 3:22–5:13).

- Worshiping God in fullness because He is not on the throne of our lives (Matt. 4:10; 15:9; John 4:23–24; 9:31; Rom. 1:23; 9:4; Col. 3:5).

- Realizing our utter impotence in the grand scope of creation and the inevitability of either giving in to God or suffering tragic earthly and eternal consequences (Job 38; Gal. 6:7–10; Phil. 2:5–10).

4. For God to complete His work in our lives, we must decide to eliminate the garbage we have chosen that keeps Him at arm's length.

Jesus told His detractors that the most important task they faced was to love God with all their heart, soul, mind, and strength (Mark 12:30–31). My research with American adults who are people on the journey to holiness emphasized the importance and accuracy of that contention. People become isolated from God and resistant to brokenness because of emotional blockages or pain (i.e., issues of the heart); spiritual ignorance, confusion, or self-indulgence (i.e., matters of the soul); intellectual distortions and misunderstandings (i.e., challenges of the mind); or behavioral and physical obstacles (i.e., manifestations of strength). Our adversary is an expert at blending potential seductions in these areas into a minefield that maims and destroys us.

However, in our moments of clarity, we might recognize the truth: we are being held back from the loving embrace of a Father who wants to heal, love, preserve, empower, release, and enjoy us. When we feel that His unyielding response to our stray behaviors and thoughts is stern, we need to realize that it is the necessary act of a loving parent who must discipline a wayward child for their own good. And we must see our difficult times as the precursor to ultimate victory in Christ. While the powers of this world have often succeeded at distorting our understanding of God's purposes, in the end, the hardships He allows are necessary and beneficial aspects of our development.

In fact, if we study God's teachings about our well-being, we cannot escape the realization that brokenness is a biblical promise and an eternal gift. We resent it because Western societies have become soft and embrace a sense of entitlement. We believe our own press about our great accomplishments and sensitivities. We seek continual comfort, abundance, security, and leisure. We deem hardships and sacrifice as unnecessary and sometimes believe they are even unfair or counterproductive. We consider pain and suffering to be avoidable and undesirable. We recoil in horror at the notion of voluntary brokenness. Our wholehearted embrace of this worldly perspective is our tangible rejection of the foundation of Jesus's model and message for us.

As far as I can tell, brokenness can take place in two ways. The first is for us to recognize the problem that mandates the need, understand what brokenness means, and will ourselves into a place of brokenness before God. This requires that we understand the consequences of our sin against God, of usurping God's authority and taking His place on the throne of power, and of taking our cues from society rather than God's Word. Cut to the heart by our callous insensitivity toward Christ and our consistent wrongdoing against a holy and loving deity, we, therefore, experience a life-shattering realization of our selfishness, independence, control, and evil. We desperately throw ourselves on God's mercy, pleading with Him to forgive our narcissistic and unrighteous behavior. We find ourselves on the threshold of depression and despair, wholly distraught over our indefensible choices and their effect on our relationship with both a loving and benevolent God as well as the people whom we are called to bless. We are virtually impotent to continue to live without God absolving us of our spiritual sickness, powerless to keep going without His willingness to walk alongside us.

Such a response is theoretically possible and is the approach that many ministries equip us to pursue. However, after conducting numerous case studies and more than eighteen thousand interviews regarding people's transformational journey, *I have yet to encounter a single individual who has successfully broken themselves.*

That leads to the second means to brokenness—allowing God to do it His way. Every case of successful brokenness I've studied has been initiated by God. He does this by allowing us to endure a life crisis. If the expression "successful brokenness" seems a bit odd, please know that it is an intentional choice of words. It refers to the fact that God often strives to work with us to facilitate our brokenness, but we usually resist, resulting in a missed opportunity to minimize ourselves and maximize God's presence and authority in our lives. Urged on by our secular society, we remain full of ourselves, leaving little room for God to be present in our lives. In fact, our worldview does not interpret life crises as examples of God at work. Rather, we view such challenges as instances of "bad luck," "chance," "unfortunate circumstances," "the circle of life," "negative karma," or "the randomness of life."

It may seem unlikely, unnecessary, or even unloving for God to expose us to harsh circumstances in order to break us. With our upbeat and optimistic theology, a view that glosses over the roles of persecution and suffering, we believe God's primary interest is in providing the best for us at all times. We explain away the hardships Moses, David, Jesus, and Paul faced. We are aghast when told God loves us so much that He allowed us to face another crisis, which He followed up with pain and suffering in all four life dimensions (emotionally, psychologically, physically, spiritually) to more perfectly shape us into His image. *How,* we wonder, *is that the work of a loving God?*

Actually, the crisis approach is a response to our refusal to work with Him any other way. It's not like He hasn't tried to get our attention through a variety of alternative means. We have left Him little choice.

- He tried to reach us emotionally through our understanding of what His own Son, Jesus Christ, went through on our behalf, including how Jesus was broken because of (our) sin.
- He used sermons and other forms of instruction in an effort to pierce our intellect.
- He used the Bible as another conduit of psychological challenge, describing His principles, commands, stories, and warnings in the form of narratives, poetry, and polemics.
- He exposed us to the suffering and hardships of others, hoping we'd learn the lesson vicariously.
- He even tried to permeate our heads and our hearts through excessive, undeserved, and frequent blessings, only to see us miss the point by taking them for granted.

You can't say God didn't go all out in His efforts to rip us out of our comfort zone in softer and gentler ways. But because we constantly resisted His efforts, He has unleashed what may well be the last resort, snapping us to attention in the same way He broke His Son: through physical hardship and anguish.

By the way, my research found that a majority of people who are finally broken experience harsh circumstances time after time after time. Why? Because the first time or two—or three or more—we take our cues from a culture that says brokenness is for weak losers. We see nothing positive emerging from those difficulties. Instead, we consider them tests that will prove our worthiness through self-reliance, independence, personal strength, and perseverance.

Sadly, we fail to learn from experience—either ours or that of others whose challenges we observe. Everyone experiences similar hardships, and we go through them repeatedly. Among the most common forms of crisis that lead to brokenness are imprisonment, debilitating illness or injury, the painful or prolonged death of a loved one, personal bankruptcy, acrimonious divorce, and the loss of possessions in a natural disaster. Countless other challenges exist as well, but the research found that a majority of people have undergone these difficulties one or more times en route to brokenness.

Society teaches us that crises are merely stumbling blocks on the path to victory; unfortunate barriers we can convert into opportunities to demonstrate our strength and determination. That mind-set causes us to have to undergo two or more of these crises before we wake up to our need for God. Or, as John 3:30 reminds us, God must become greater and greater in our lives, and we must become less and less.

It is also intriguing that most Christians interpret the reoccurrence of crises as a sign of God's disinterest, punishment, lack of engagement, or inability to protect us rather than as evidence of His involvement, love, care, and concern. This perspective reflects the heart of our worldview—one that is not so much Bible-centric as unrealistic and secular in nature. While the Scriptures talk about the centrality of discipline and the refining fire, we cling to a God who shields us from any painful experiences that might help us grow in our relationship with Him. Consequently, when we get beaten down by life, we question God's love and power. We assume He has abandoned us or remains indifferent to our plight.

That perspective misses the point. God's goal is not to break our spirits but to break our rebelliousness and independence. We met His less-debilitating efforts to guide us with indifference or rejection. Ironically, our continued perseverance in the face of crises meant to break us just produces additional suffering and doubt. It need not be so hard, of course. The Lord has provided a simpler and easier way out for us, if we are willing to do things His way. So, I implore you to take a serious inventory of your life and determine whether you have allowed God to break you of your addiction to sin, self, and society. If you have—you have been able to surrender your life and submit your agenda to Him and have then moved on to loving people and Him completely—praise Him for that transformation! If you have not, the only thing standing in your way is you. Once you are "successfully broken," you will be able to influence and guide society to a better place.

Worldview

It's an awesome challenge to discern God's vision for your life and allow Him to transform you so you can influence the world with His wisdom and love. The factor that will round out your capacity to be an effective change agent is a biblical worldview so that your decision-making will not veer away from the vision and purposes God has given to you.

Life is about making choices. Each of us makes hundreds of choices every day, some of which are more memorable than others or have a greater impact than others, but every one of those choices matters. Likewise, none of those choices are made in a vacuum. Each one is tied to a larger perspective on life: your worldview.

A worldview is a mental and spiritual lens through which we interpret reality. Our worldview is the filter we use to put things into context and facilitate an appropriate response. It enables us to make sense of the world by organizing information and allowing us to make choices consistent with what we believe to be true and significant. That worldview enables us to distinguish right from wrong, good from bad, useful from useless, and appropriate from inappropriate.

This is not simply an academic exercise. Everybody has a world-view—we have to have one in order to put everything we experience into perspective and to respond in a manner that is consistent with who we are and what we believe. Our worldview drives what we do because we take action based on what we believe. Every behavior is a direct outgrowth of our worldview.

Many different worldviews reflect the combination of perceptions and beliefs that people have developed. The most common worldview in America today is postmodernism, which is unbiblical in most of its foundations. The alternative is to develop a *biblical* worldview, which is a means of experiencing, interpreting, and responding to reality in relation to biblical principles and narratives. If we embrace a biblical worldview, then our every thought, word, and deed can be consistent with God's principles and commands.

In essence, possessing and living in concert with a biblical world-view provides us with the capacity to think like Jesus, in order to then act like Jesus. Blending a biblical worldview with the pursuit of transformation results in Christlike living. We must think like Jesus before we can act like Jesus, and we must be saved, broken, surrendered, and submitted in order to love God and others fully.

As noted above, everyone has a worldview that drives their decision-making. Very few people have a pure worldview—that is, purely postmodern or existentialist or nihilist or biblical or pantheistic or secular humanist or any other variety. Almost all of us have spent so little time thinking about the development and substance of our worldview—and the many messages we receive every day through advertising, entertainment, conversations, religions, and the like—that we create a syncretistic perspective. In other words, we tend to latch on to divergent worldview elements from a variety of places, creating a worldview mash-up that does not reflect any single worldview but, rather, constitutes elements from many views that are combined into something we feel comfortable with.

Earlier in this book I noted that fewer than 10 percent of born-again Christians in the United States possess a biblical worldview, and fewer than one out of every twenty Americans has adopted a biblical worldview. This is a major reason why America does not behave biblically in so many instances: the philosophy of life that dictates our responses to circumstances is not in sync with God's principles.

I, along with many others, have written entire books on how to root the cultural garbage out of our minds and hearts and replace that with the godly principles that will steer us right.[6] It is not an overnight process. It demands our full commitment. But it can be done, as evidenced by the fact that almost one out of every ten Christ followers in the United States currently possesses such a worldview, and by the fact that God calls us to have the mind of Christ (Deut. 6:2–9; Prov. 2:2–8; 3:5–7; Eccles. 12:13–14; Isa. 55:8; Rom. 12:2; 2 Cor. 10:3–5; Col. 2:8).

The essence of the worldview model I have discovered to be most effective is to pose and answer deceptively simple questions for which the Bible has answers. Responding to practical questions, rather than memorizing the doctrinal statements, makes us think. So, consider what would happen if you were to start out by answering these seven questions:

1. Does God exist?
2. What is the character and nature of God?
3. How and why was the world created?
4. What is the nature and purpose of humanity?
5. What happens after we die on this earth?
6. What spiritual authorities exist?
7. What is truth?

The key to your answers is not simply to provide a biblically defensible direct answer; it is also to explain why your biblically consistent answers matter. In other words, once you answer one of these questions, can you then answer, "So what?" That follow-up response begins to make the theological truths that answer the initial inquiry tangibly meaningful to your life—and influential in the lives of others.

Does this really matter? Will developing a biblical worldview make such a big difference in your life that it will justify the time and effort required to think like Jesus? Absolutely! Besides the fact that God commands us to think this way—which should be a sufficient reason to move each of us to do so—check out some of the data indicating the gap in behavior between those who do and those who do not have a biblical worldview.[7] Those who have a biblical worldview are:

- 12 times less likely to engage in extramarital sex
- 9 times more likely to avoid adult-only material on the internet
- 8 times less likely to gamble
- 5 times more likely to believe that Satan is real, not just a symbol of evil
- 5 times less likely to believe the Bible, the Koran, and the Book of Mormon are simply different expressions of same truths
- 4 times more likely to reject the idea that a person can reach Heaven through personal goodness or doing good works
- 3 times more likely to affirm the holiness of Jesus Christ
- 3 times more likely to intentionally not watch a movie/video because they know it contains objectionable content
- 3 times less likely to get drunk
- 3 times more likely to pray for the president
- 3 times more likely to read the Bible, other than at church services or events
- 3 times more likely to believe the Bible describes homosexuality as sinful
- 2.5 times more likely to believe the Bible is totally accurate in all the principles it teaches
- 2 times more likely to volunteer time to help the needy

Imagine what American society would be like if more people had a biblical worldview. No, it would not be perfect, and sin would still be rampant. But we would be on a path toward greater righteousness, justice, holiness, and love.

Directing the nation onto that pathway starts with you.

The Bottom Line

Ultimately, then, the answer to the core question of this section—What can you do?—hinges on your willingness to become the person God created you to be in order to have the influence He has granted to you for such a time as this. Your responsibility is to understand His vision for your life, see it through His eyes and values (i.e., a biblical worldview), and then implement that vision as a transformed, Christlike servant of the eternal King.

Our nation can be restored only by God. But He accomplishes His ends through the people, like you and me, whom He created to carry out limited and specific—but necessary and important—roles in the renewal of America. That renewal depends entirely on each of us fulfilling our designated purpose to produce God's desires. Armed with free will, it is our choice to serve Him in this way. But our choices have consequences, and to date, most American Christians have chosen to follow their own desires rather than those of God. Similarly, the local church has not risen to the occasion, failing to be the guiding and restorative presence it is called to be.

And that's why we're in the mess we find ourselves in today. It's a lot to think about, isn't it? But such reflection is time well spent. The Teacher reminds us, "How wonderful to be wise, to analyze and interpret things" (Eccles. 8:1). Indeed, this age calls for the wisdom of those who trust in the Lord for true understanding rather than rely on their own intelligence and instincts.

You may be a bit put off by my emphasis on getting your life in concert with God's expectations, rather than including a "solutions" chapter on how we can make demands of other people in order to fix the world. Granted, America's society needs lots of fixing! But the solutions must start with you and me. In the same way that Jesus instructed His followers to remove the log in their own eye before tinkering with the speck in someone else's eye, we have no right to judge the choices and behavior of others until we get our lives straightened up (Matt. 7:4–5).

So, the initial course of action we must take—our emphasis on commitment and wisdom-driven action—must be to ascertain God's unique vision for us, to understand how that intersects His vision for His people, and to allow the Lord to transform us into the people He made us to be, people who will transform society by loving other people into His presence and ways.

Having a plan of action without executing it is folly. God gently reminds us that "wise words bring many benefits, and hard work brings rewards" (Prov. 12:14). Wisdom without action is just clever ideas. May you discover the wisdom needed to facilitate the activity that renews your life, restores America, and blesses the Lord.

If not you, then who?

If not now, then when?

If not renewal, then what?

I'll see you on the front lines.

APPENDIX

ABOUT THE AMERICAN CULTURE & FAITH INSTITUTE

The American Culture & Faith Institute (ACFI) is the public opinion research arm of United in Purpose (UiP), a nonprofit organization based in Northern California. ACFI is a nonpartisan, not-for-profit research entity. Under the guidance of researcher George Barna, ACFI conducts surveys throughout the year, interviewing theologically conservative Protestant pastors and politically conservative Christian adults (both Protestant and Catholic) to gauge the sentiment and activity of conservatives. The research is used to assist UiP's partner organizations in understanding cultural trends, developing planning and outreach efforts, increasing the awareness and engagement of Christians in the political arena, helping to facilitate higher voter turnout among Christians, exerting influence for positive cultural change, educating the public and media about conservatives and their perspectives, informing church leaders about the people they serve, and assisting theologically conservative churches in advancing a biblical worldview. ACFI surveys are conducted by telephone and online. Some of its work is accessible online at www.culturefaith.com.

ACFI examines the opinions and behavior of conservatives through its branded tracking research: the RightView and C-3 research projects.

RightView™

This is a longitudinal survey in which a panel of more than 25,000 adults who are politically conservative and spiritually active are studied. The primary group within this base is known as SAGE Cons—Spiritually Active Governance Engaged Conservatives. This is the only longitudinal study of its kind in the United States. Each survey examines divergent aspects of American culture, faith, and politics based on interviews with a minimum of one thousand qualified individuals per study.

Since its inception in 2012, ACFI has conducted dozens of Right-View surveys, providing invaluable insight to UiP's numerous organizational partners who are engaged in motivating, educating, and activating conservatives across America.

C-3 Research

C-3 is an abbreviation for Conservative Clergy Canvass™. This is a longitudinal survey in which clergy from a panel of more than 10,000 theologically conservative senior pastors of Protestant churches are regularly interviewed. These pastors are a representative sample of the estimated 90,000–105,000 Protestant churches in America that are theologically conservative—roughly one-third of the nation's Protestant churches. This is the only longitudinal study of its kind in the United States. Each survey examines divergent aspects of American culture, faith, and politics.

Since the launch of ACFI, surveys have been regularly conducted among this vital group of church leaders. The results of this research have been shared with UiP's organizational partners to enhance their joint efforts at motivating, educating, and activating theologically conservative pastors and their congregations across America.

United in Purpose

United in Purpose (a 501[c]4 organization) and United in Purpose–Education (a 501[c]3 entity) share a critical mission: to provide information and resources intended to help people understand and embrace a biblical worldview and to encourage them to live accordingly. UiP endeavors to accomplish that end by working with, uniting, and equipping like-minded conservative organizations to bring biblical values to the forefront in homes, schools, churches, businesses, the media, and the public arena. What UiP brings to the table in that effort is the provision of technology, research, relationships, and marketing strategies geared toward facilitating cultural change in America based on Judeo-Christian principles. UiP believes that when Americans live in concert with God's principles, as described in the Bible, American culture and individual lives will be transformed for the better. On the political continuum, UiP supports conservative principles but is nonpartisan.

SOURCES

Ayres, Whit. *2016 and Beyond: How Republicans Can Elect a President in the New America*. Washington, DC: Resurgent Republic, 2015.

Barna, George. *Maximum Faith: Live Like Jesus*. New York: SGG Publishing, 2011.

———. *The Seven Faith Tribes: Who They Are, What They Believe, and Why They Matter*. Carol Stream, IL: Tyndale, 2011.

Barna, George, and David Barton. *U-Turn: Restoring America to the Strength of Its Roots*. Lake Mary, FL: Frontline, 2014.

Barna, George, and David Kinnaman. *Churchless: Understanding Today's Unchurched and How to Connect with Them*. Carol Stream, IL: Tyndale, 2014.

Bok, Sissela. *Exploring Happiness: From Aristotle to Brain Science*. New Haven, CT: Yale University Press, 2011.

Brooks, Arthur. *Gross National Happiness: Why Happiness Matters for America—and How We Can Get More of It*. New York: Basic Books, 2008.

Diaz-Ortiz, Claire. *Greater Expectations: Succeed (and Stay Sane) in an On-Demand, All-Access, Always-On Age*. Grand Rapids: Zondervan, 2014.

Dickerson, John. *The Great Evangelical Recession: 6 Factors That Will Crash the American Church . . . and How to Prepare*. Grand Rapids: Baker Books, 2013.

Douthat, Ross. *Bad Religion: How We Became a Nation of Heretics*. New York: Free Press, 2012.

Easterbrook, Gregg. *The Progress Paradox: How Life Gets Better While People Feel Worse*. New York: Random House, 2003.

Friedman, George. *The Next Decade: Empire and Republic in a Changing World*. New York: Anchor Books, 2012.

————. *The Next 100 Years*. Doubleday: New York, 2009.

Gingrich, Newt, and Nancy Desmond. *The Art of Transformation*. Washington, DC: CHT Press, 2006.

Himmelfarb, Gertrude. *One Nation, Two Cultures*. New York: Alfred Knopf, 1999.

Kim, David. *Twenty and Something: Have the Time of Your Life (and Figure It All Out Too)*. Grand Rapids: Zondervan, 2013.

Kinnaman, David. *You Lost Me: Why Young Christians Are Leaving the Church . . . and Rethinking Faith*. Grand Rapids: Baker Books, 2011.

Kinnaman, David, and Gabe Lyons. *UnChristian: What a Generation Really Thinks about Christianity . . . and Why It Matters*. Grand Rapids: Baker Books, 2007.

Kohut, Andrew, and Bruce Stokes. *America against the World: How We Are Different and Why We Are Disliked*. New York: Times Books, 2006.

Luntz, Frank. *What Americans Really Want . . . Really: The Truth about Our Hopes, Dreams, and Fears*. New York: Hyperion, 2009.

Marsden, Peter, ed. *Social Trends in American Life: Findings from the General Social Survey since 1972*. Princeton, NJ: Princeton University Press, 2012.

Newport, Frank. *God Is Alive and Well: The Future of Religion in America*. New York: Gallup Press, 2012.

Nuttle, Marc. *Moment of Truth: How Our Government's Addiction to Spending and Power Will Destroy Everything That Makes America Great*. Lake Mary, FL: Frontline, 2008.

O'Malley, John. *Four Cultures of the West*. Cambridge, MA: Harvard University Press, 2004.

Rath, Tom, and Jim Harter. *Wellbeing: The Five Essential Elements*. New York: Gallup Press, 2010.

Schama, Simon. *The American Future: A History*. New York: Ecco, 2009.

Silver, Nate. *The Signal and the Noise: Why So Many Predictions Fail—but Some Don't*. New York: Penguin, 2012.

Taylor, Paul, and Pew Research Center. *The Next America: Boomers, Millennials, and the Looming Generational Showdown*. New York: PublicAffairs, 2014.

Tyson, Jon. *Sacred Roots: Why Church Still Matters in a Post-Religious Era*. Grand Rapids: Zondervan, 2013.

Zakaria, Fareed. *The Post-American World*. New York: Norton & Company, 2008.

NOTES

Chapter 1 Religious Beliefs

1. Barna Group, OmniPoll™1-05, national survey of 1,003 adults, conducted January 2005; Barna Group, OmniPoll™1-15C, national survey of 2,002 adults, conducted January 2015.

2. Barna Group, OmniPoll™1-15C, national survey of 2,002 adults, conducted January 2015.

3. Data based on Frames W2, a national survey of 1,414 adults, conducted June 2013 by the Barna Group.

4. Ibid.

5. Barna Group, OmniPoll™1-05, national survey of 1,003 adults, conducted January 2005; Barna Group, OmniPoll™1-15C, national survey of 2,002 adults, conducted January 2015.

6. Barna Group, OmniPoll™1-15C, national survey of 2,002 adults, conducted January 2015.

7. Ibid.

8. Ibid.

9. Ibid.

Chapter 2 Religious Behavior

1. Information based on national surveys, including Frames W1, national survey of 1,086 adults, conducted by Barna Group, May 2013; OmniPoll™1-13OL, national survey of 1,078 adults, conducted by Barna Group, January 2013; and data described in George Barna and David Kinnaman, *Churchless: Understanding Today's Unchurched and How to Connect with Them* (Carol Stream, IL: Tyndale, 2014), chap. 2, 5.

2. Barna Group, OmniPoll™1-15C, national survey of 2,002 adults, conducted January 2015.

3. Sources include the following national surveys conducted by the Barna Group: OmniPoll™ 1-12OL, national survey of 1,005 adults, conducted March 2012; Frames W3, national survey of 1,000 adults, conducted August 2013; Barna Group, OmniPoll™ 1-14OL, national survey of 1,024 adults, conducted February 2014; Frames W1, national survey of

1,086 adults, conducted May 2013; and Barna Group, OmniPoll™1-13OL, national survey of 1,078 adults, conducted January 2013.

4. Barna Group, OmniPoll™1-04, national survey of 1,003 adults, conducted January 2004; Barna Group, OmniPoll™1-14C, national survey of 2,036 adults, conducted February 2014.

5. Barna Group, OmniPoll™1-15C, national survey of 2,002 adults, conducted January 2015.

6. Barna Group, OmniPoll™1-05, national survey of 1,003 adults, conducted January 2005; Barna Group, OmniPoll™1-15C, national survey of 2,002 adults, conducted January 2015.

7. Barna Group, OmniPoll™1-13OL, national survey of 1,078 adults, conducted January 2013.

8. Barna Group, Frames W3, national survey of 1,000 adults, conducted August 2013.

9. Barna Group, OmniPoll™ 1-15C, national survey of 2,002 adults, conducted January 2015.

10. The question used to determine such participation has been refined over time by the Barna Group before settling on the following wording, used since 2006: "Some people are part of a group of believers that meets regularly in a home or place other than a church building. These groups are not part of a typical church; they meet independently, are self-governed, and consider themselves to be a complete church on their own. Do you participate in such a group, sometimes known as a house church or simple church, that is *not* part of a local, congregational type of church?" The data are drawn from the following Barna Group studies: OmniPoll™ 1-14OL, national survey of 1,024 adults, conducted February 2014; OmniPoll™ 2-06/F-06, national survey of 2,008 adults, conducted August–October 2006.

Chapter 3 The Unchurched

1. For a comprehensive, research-based understanding of the unchurched population, see George Barna and David Kinnaman, *Churchless: Understanding Today's Unchurched and How to Connect with Them* (Carol Stream, IL: Tyndale, 2014).

2. Barna Group, OmniPoll™ 1-13™, national survey of 898 unchurched adults, conducted January 2013.

3. For a more extensive discussion about how to increase people's openness to a conventional church experience, see Barna and Kinnaman, *Churchless*. Chapter 13, in particular, delves into this issue.

Chapter 4 Religious Education

1. Based on the annual OmniPoll™ tracking surveys conducted by the Barna Group since 1984. Each of these national surveys includes interviews with a national random sample of adults of a minimum of 1,000 people.

2. American Association of Publishers annual reports; proprietary report by Statista; proprietary research by Metaformation; Book Industry Study Group; and US Bureau of the Census.

3. American Culture & Faith Institute, RightView-9 and RightView-10, national surveys conducted in September–October 2014, N=3,272. Also, Barna Group, OmniPoll™ 1-95, January 1995, N=1,006; OmniPoll™ 1-05, January 2005, N=1,003; OmniPoll™ 1-15OL, N=969.

4. American Faith & Culture Institute, *God's People Want to Know* (Woodside, CA, August 2015), http://www.culturefaith.com/wp-content/uploads/2015/09/Gods-People-Want-to-Know-Barna-ACFI_8-27-15.pdf.

5. Ibid.

6. Ibid.

7. Barna Group, OmniPoll™ 1-13, a national survey of adults, N=2,083.

8. Data from RightView-13, a national survey among 1,913 spiritually active and politically conservative adults conducted in December 2014 by American Culture & Faith Institute, Woodside, CA.

9. Based on a comparison of data from the Barna Group annual study of faith in the United States: OmniPoll™ 1-95, conducted January 1995, N=1.006; OmniPoll™ 1-05, conducted January 2005, N=1,003; OmniPoll™ 1-15C, conducted January 2015, N=2,002.

10. Ibid.

11. Ibid.

12. Ibid.

13. Ibid.

14. American Faith & Culture Institute, *God's People*.

15. Barna Group, OmniPoll™ 1-14, conducted January 2014, N=2,036; OmniPoll™ 1-13, conducted January 2013, N=2,083.

Chapter 5 The Bible

1. Barna Group, OmniPoll™ 1-13PH, N=1,005, conducted January 2013; Barna Group, OmniPoll™ 1-15PH, N=1,010, conducted January 2015.

2. Barna Group, OmniPoll™ 1-15PH, N=1,010, conducted January 2015, questions commissioned by the American Bible Society.

3. Barna Group, OmniPoll™ 1-15C, N=2,002, conducted January 2015.

4. Ibid.

5. Barna Group, OmniPoll™ 1-13OL, N=1,078, conducted January 2013, questions commissioned by the American Bible Society.

6. Barna Group, OmniPoll™ 1-13PH, N=1,005, conducted January 2013, questions commissioned by the American Bible Society.

7. Barna Group, OmniPoll™ 1-15C, N=2,002, conducted January 2015; Barna Group, OmniPoll™ 1-10, N=1,005, conducted January 2010.

8. Barna Group, OmniPoll™ 1-13PH, N=1,005, conducted January 2013; OmniPoll™ 1-15PH, N=1,010, conducted January 2015; OmniPoll™ F-14OL, N=1,036, conducted September 2014. These data are from questions commissioned by the American Bible Society.

9. Ibid.

10. Barna Group, OmniPoll™ 1-15PH, N=1,010, conducted January 2015, questions commissioned by the American Bible Society.

11. Ibid.

12. Barna Group, OmniPoll™ 1-15C, N=2,002, conducted January 2015.

13. Barna Group, OmniPoll™ 1-13OL, N=1,078, conducted January 2013, questions commissioned by the American Bible Society.

14. Barna Group, OmniPoll™ 1-15PH, N=1,010, conducted January 2015, questions commissioned by the American Bible Society.

15. Barna Group, OmniPoll™ 1-13OL, N=1,078, conducted January 2013, questions commissioned by the American Bible Society.

16. Barna Group, OmniPoll™ 1-13PH, N=1,005, conducted January 2013, questions commissioned by the American Bible Society.

17. Barna Group, OmniPoll™ 1-15C, N=2,002, conducted January 2015; Barna Group, OmniPoll™ 1-10, N=1,005, conducted January 2010.

18. Barna Group, OmniPoll™ 1-15C, N=2,002, conducted January 2015.

19. Barna Group, OmniPoll™ 1-13OL, N=1,078, conducted January 2013, questions commissioned by the American Bible Society.

20. Barna Group, OmniPoll™ 1-15PH, N=1,010, conducted January 2015, questions commissioned by the American Bible Society.

21. Ibid.

22. Ibid.

Chapter 6 Evangelicals

1. Throughout this book, I will refer to evangelicals as defined by the Barna Group's research. Thirty years ago we pioneered a way of evaluating faith segments based on their theological beliefs rather than self-identification. (Our subsequent testing of those disparate approaches revealed a massive disconnect between people's self-reported labels and their theological beliefs, strengthening our resolve to continue to measure faith segments based on theology.) Among Christians, my research typically refers to three different segments: evangelicals, non-evangelical born agains, and notionals. All born-again Christians say they have made a personal commitment to Jesus Christ that is still important in their lives today and that when they die they know they will go to Heaven but only because they have confessed their sins and accepted Jesus Christ as their Savior. Not only are evangelicals born again, but they also embrace seven other theological perspectives: (1) their religious faith is very important in their lives; (2) they have a personal responsibility to share the gospel with nonbelievers; (3) they strongly believe the Bible is totally accurate in all the principles it teaches; (4) they strongly believe Jesus Christ lived a sinless life; (5) they strongly reject the idea that Satan is not a living entity but only a symbol of evil; (6) they strongly reject the notion that a good person—or one who does enough good works—can earn a place in Heaven; (7) and they define the God they believe in as the all-knowing, all-powerful Creator of the universe who still rules that universe today. By definition, born-again Christians may believe one or more of these but not all of them. Notional Christians do not accept the born-again criteria but consider themselves to be Christian. In this book, if no adjective is used to distinguish which type of born-again Christians are being referenced—that is, just the non-evangelical born agains as distinct from all born agains (which would include evangelicals), then you may assume I am speaking about all born-again Christians.

2. Barna Group, OmniPoll™1-15C, national survey of 2,002 adults, conducted January 2015; Barna Group, OmniPoll™ 1-14C, national survey of 2,036 adults, conducted February 2014; Barna Group, OmniPoll™1-13OL, national survey of 1,078 adults, conducted January 2013.

3. Ibid.

4. Ibid.

5. Ibid.

6. Center for the Study of American Faith & Culture, *The Role of Faith in the 2012 Presidential Vote*, published March 1, 2013, http://www.culturefaith.com/wp-content/uploads /2013/08/Role-of-Faith_2012_Presidential-Vote_Culture-Faith-Min.pdf.

7. This based on the annual tracking study by the Barna Group, conducted every January among a national random sample of adults that ranges in size from 1,000 to 3,000 people. These surveys have been conducted every year since 1985.

8. American Culture & Faith Institute, RightView-13, a national survey of conservative adults, N=1,839, conducted December 2014.

9. This concept is especially evident in the American context during the great spiritual awakenings or revivals in the nation's past. More insight into the dynamics of such spiritual growth can be found in Nathan Hatch, *The Democratization of American Christianity*

(New Haven, CT: Yale University Press, 1991); Michael Corbett, Julia Corbett-Hemeyer, and J. Matthew Wilson, *Politics and Religion in the United States* (New York: Routledge, 2013); Sydney Ahlstrom, *A Religious History of the American People* (New Haven, CT: Yale University Press, 2004). Other helpful sources regarding American history and religious faith are www.wallbuilders.com and its sister ministry, www.blackrobereg.org.

Chapter 7 Life Transformation

1. The information in this summary is drawn from a multiphase research project conducted over the course of six years in which people's spiritual lives were traced and analyzed to determine the typical journey people experience. That journey is described in detail in George Barna, *Maximum Faith: Live Like Jesus* (Ventura, CA: Metaformation, 2011). The study entailed interviews with more than 17,000 adults, and core factors in the research have been updated since then, most recently in 2015.

2. Barna, *Maximum Faith*. Data updated from Barna Group, OmniPoll™ 1-15C, N=2,002, conducted January 2015.

3. Ibid.

4. Ibid.

5. Ibid.

6. Ibid.

7. Ibid.

8. Ibid.

9. Barna Group, OmniPoll™ 1-13OL, N=1,078, conducted January 2013.

10. Barna Group, Frames W2, a national survey of 1,414 adults, conducted June 2013.

11. Ibid.

12. Barna Group, OmniPoll™ F-14C, N=2,005, conducted December 2014.

Chapter 8 Government Satisfaction

1. Gallup Organization monthly tracking of satisfaction with the way things are going in this country has revealed that less than one-third of the public has been satisfied since late 2012. See http://pollingreport.com/right.htm.

2. Hart Research Associates and Public Opinion Strategies research conducted monthly shows that since the beginning of 2013, fewer than one-third of adults have believed the nation is headed in the right direction. See http://pollingreport.com/right.htm.

3. "Trust in Government," Gallup, last accessed February 4, 2016, http://www.gallup.com/poll/5392/trust-government.aspx.

4. Pew Research Center, *2014 Political Polarization and Typology Survey*, 2014, http://www.people-press.org/files/2014/06/2014-06-26-Appendix-4-Typology-Topline.pdf.

5. Barna Group, Frames W3, national survey of 1,000 adults, conducted August 2013; Aaron Blake, "How Much Do People Hate Congress? Let Us Count the Ways," *Washington Post*, August 4, 2014, citing a *CBS News/New York Times* survey about the public's distrust of Congress, http://www.washingtonpost.com/news/the-fix/wp/2014/08/04/how-much-do-people-hate-congress-let-us-count-the-ways/.

6. Justin McCarthy, "Americans Name Government as No. 1 US Problem," Gallup, March 12, 2015, http://www.gallup.com/poll/181946/americans-name-government-no-problem.aspx.

7. Frank Newport, "Most in US Still Proud to Be an American," Gallup, July 4, 2013, http://www.gallup.com/poll/163361/proud-american.aspx.

8. Frank Newport, "Views in US That Gov't Is Too Powerful Show Little Change," Gallup, May 27, 2013, http://www.gallup.com/poll/162779/views-gov-powerful-little-changed

.aspx?utm_source=rights%20and%20freedoms&utm_medium=search&utm_campaign =tiles.

9. Public Policy Polling, "Congress Less Popular than Cockroaches, Traffic Jams," news release, January 8, 2013, http://www.publicpolicypolling.com/pdf/2011/PPP_Release_Natl _010813_.pdf.

10. Rebecca Riffkin, "Americans Say Federal Gov't Wastes 51 Cents on the Dollar," Gallup, September 17, 2014, http://www.gallup.com/poll/176102/americans-say-federal-gov -wastes-cents-dollar.aspx?utm_source=state%20government&utm_medium=search&utm _campaign=tiles.

11. Jeffrey M. Jones, "Americans Remain Divided on Preference for Gov't Activity," Gallup, September 29, 2014, http://www.gallup.com/poll/177422/americans-remain-divided -preference-gov-activity.aspx?utm_source=government%20doing%20too%20many%20 things&utm_medium=search&utm_campaign=tiles; Pew, *2014 Survey*.

12. Rebecca Riffkin, "Satisfaction with US Governance Lower than Pre-Shutdown," Gallup, September 24, 2014, http://www.gallup.com/poll/177308/satisfaction-governance-lower -pre-shutdown.aspx?utm_source=governed&utm_medium=search&utm_campaign=tiles.

13. Rebecca Riffkin, "Americans Rate Nurses Highest on Honesty, Ethical Standards," Gallup, December 18, 2014, http://www.gallup.com/poll/180260/americans-rate-nurses -highest-honesty-ethical-standards.aspx?utm_source=ethical%20standards&utm_medium =search&utm_campaign=tiles.

14. Barna Group, Frames W3, national survey of 1,000 adults, conducted August 2013.

15. Pew, *2014 Survey*.

16. See the Political Figures section, by name of the figure in question, at http://www .pollingreport.com/A-B.htm. Also, explore the ratings of the president and other major office holders using the index at the Pollingreport.com home page.

17. Alexander Hess, "The Ten Largest Employers in America," *USA Today*, August 22, 2013, http://www.usatoday.com/story/money/business/2013/08/22/ten-largest-employers /2680249/; US Office of Personnel Management, "Data, Analysis, and Documentation," Washington, DC, https://www.opm.gov/policy-data-oversight/data-analysis-documentation/federal -employment-reports/historical-tables/total-government-employment-since-1962/.

18. Pew, *2014 Survey*; Barna Group, Frames W3, national survey of 1,000 adults, conducted August 2013.

19. Rebecca Riffkin, "Americans Say Federal Government Wastes Fifty-One Cents on the Dollar," Gallup, September 17, 2014, http://www.gallup.com/poll/176102/americans-say -federal-gov-wastes-cents-dollar.aspx?utm_source=state%20government&utm_medium =search&utm_campaign=tiles.

20. Pew, *2014 Survey*.

21. Ibid.

22. Ibid.

23. Ibid.

24. Ibid.

25. Barna Group, Frames W3, national survey of 1,000 adults, conducted August 2013.

26. Ibid.

27. Ibid.

Chapter 9 Political Engagement

1. Thom File, *Who Votes? Congressional Elections and the American Electorate: 1978– 2014*, US Census Bureau (Washington, DC, July 2015), http://www.census.gov/content/dam /Census/library/publications/2015/demo/p20-577.pdf.

2. "2014 November General Election Turnout Rates," United States Election Project, last updated December 30, 2015, http://www.electproject.org/2014g.

3. Ibid.

4. Jeffrey M. Jones, "Voter Engagement Lower than in 2010 and 2006 Midterms," Gallup, October 8, 2014, http://www.gallup.com/poll/178130/voter-engagement-lower-2010-2 006-midterms.aspx?utm_source=political%20engagement&utm_medium=search&utm _campaign=tiles.

5. Pew Research Center, "Section 5: Political Activism and Engagement," *Political Polarization in the American Public*, June 12, 2014, http://www.people-press.org/2014/06/12/section -5-political-engagement-and-activism/; Pew Research Center, "Table 5.1 Political Engagement," June 12, 2014, http://www.people-press.org/2014/06/12/political-engagement-table/.

6. Aaron Smith, "Civic Engagement in the Digital Age," Pew Research Center, April 25, 2013, http://www.pewinternet.org/2013/04/25/civic-engagement-in-the-digital-age/.

7. Ibid.

8. File, *Who Votes?*

9. "Voter Turnout," United States Election Project, last accessed January 20, 2016, http:// www.electproject.org/home/voter-turnout/voter-turnout-data.

10. Ibid.

11. Ibid.

12. Ibid.

13. Ibid.

14. Pew, "Political Activism and Engagement"; Pew, "Table 5.1"; Smith, "Civic Engagement."

15. Luca Ferrini, "Why Is Turnout at Elections Declining Across the Democratic World?" E-International Relations Students, September 27, 2012, http://www.e-ir.info/2012/09/27/ why-is-turnout-at-elections-declining-across-the-democratic-world/; American Culture & Faith Institute, RightView-11, N=201 November 2014.

16. Ferrini, "Why Is Turnout at Elections Declining?"

Chapter 10 Political Ideology

1. Henry Enten, "There Are More Liberals, But Not Fewer Conservatives," FiveThirtyEight, June 10, 2015, http://fivethirtyeight.com/datalab/there-are-more-liberals-but-not -fewer-conservatives/; Lydia Saad, "US Liberals at Record 24 Percent, but Still Trail Conservatives," Gallup, January 9, 2015, http://www.gallup.com/poll/180452/liberals-record-trail -conservatives.aspx; Barna Group, OmniPoll™ 1-15, N=2,002, January 2015.

2. Ibid.

3. Ibid.

4. Ibid.

5. Ibid.

6. Jeffrey M. Jones, "In US, New Record 43 Percent Are Political Independents," Gallup Poll, January 7, 2015, http://www.gallup.com/poll/180440/new-record-political-independents. aspx?utm_source=party%20affiliation&utm_medium=search&utm_campaign=tiles; Andrew Dugan, "Democratic Party Reclaims Edge in Favorable Ratings," Gallup, July 20, 2015, http://www.gallup.com/poll/184214/democratic-party-reclaims-edge-favorable-ratings .aspx?utm_source=party%20favorability&utm_medium=search&utm_campaign=tiles.

7. Based on six national surveys with Christian adults, encompassing 9,924 interviews. The surveys were conducted November 2014–July 2015.

8. Pew Research Center, "Appendix A: The Ideological Consistency Scale," *Political Polarization in the American Public*, June 12, 2014, http://www.people-press.org/2014/06/12/appendix-a-the-ideological-consistency-scale/.

9. Based on national surveys of adults conducted by Pew Research Center: conducted September 2013, N=1,005; August 2014, N= 2,002; December 2014, N=1,507; and September 2015, N=1,502.

10. Jeffrey M. Jones, "US Baby Boomers More Likely to Identify as Conservative," Gallup, January 29, 2015, http://www.gallup.com/poll/181325/baby-boomers-likely-identify-conservative.aspx?g_source=.

Chapter 11 National Priorities

1. "Most Important Problem," Gallup, last accessed January 21, 2016, http://www.gallup.com/poll/1675/Most-Important-Problem.aspx; Bruce Drake, "State of the Union 2015: How Americans See the Nation, Their Leaders, and the Issues," Pew Research Center, January 20, 2015, http://www.pewresearch.org/fact-tank/2015/01/20/state-of-the-union-2015/; "Public's Policy Priorities Reflect Changing Conditions at Home and Abroad," Pew Research Center, January 15, 2015, http://www.people-press.org/2015/01/15/publics-policy-priorities-reflect-changing-conditions-at-home-and-abroad/#views-of-importance-of-environmental-protection-global-warming.

2. Rebecca Riffkin, "Government, Economy, Immigration Seen as Top US Problems," Gallup, September 17, 2015, http://www.gallup.com/poll/185504/government-economy-immigration-seen-top-problems.aspx?g_source=top%20US%20problems&g_medium=search&g_campaign=tiles; Rebecca Riffkin, "Mentions of Terrorism Rise as US Most Important Problem," Gallup, February 18, 2015, http://www.gallup.com/poll/181619/mentions-terrorism-rise-important-problem.aspx?g_source=top%20US%20problems&g_medium=search&g_campaign=tiles; Rebecca Riffkin, "Mentions of Jobs as Top US Problem at Six-Year Low," Gallup, January 14, 2015, http://www.gallup.com/poll/181136/mentions-jobs-top-problem-six-year-low.aspx?g_source=top%20US%20problems&g_medium=search&g_campaign=tiles; Rebecca Riffkin, "Americans Say Government, Economy Most Important Problems," Gallup, November 12, 2014, http://www.gallup.com/poll/179381/americans-say-government-economy-important-problems.aspx?g_source=top%20US%20problems&g_medium=search&g_campaign=tiles; Rebecca Riffkin, "Since 9/11, Fewer Americans Say Terrorism Top Problem," Gallup, September 10, 2014, http://www.gallup.com/poll/175721/fewer-americans-say-terrorism-top-problem.aspx?g_source=top%20US%20problems&g_medium=search&g_campaign=tiles; Andrew Dugan, "In US, Syria Emerges as a Top Problem, but Trails Economy," Gallup, September 11, 2013, http://www.gallup.com/poll/164348/syria-emerges-top-problem-trails-economy.aspx?g_source=top%20US%20problems&g_medium=search&g_campaign=tiles; Frank Newport, "Few in US See Guns, Immigration as Nation's Top Problems," Gallup, April 15, 2013, http://www.gallup.com/poll/161813/few-guns-immigration-nation-top-problems.aspx?g_source=top%20US%20problems&g_medium=search&g_campaign=tiles; Frank Newport, "Debt, Gov't Dysfunction Rise to Top of Americans' Issue List," Gallup, January 14, 2013, http://www.gallup.com/poll/159830/debt-gov-dysfunction-rise-top-americans-issue-list.aspx?g_source=top%20US%20problems&g_medium=search&g_campaign=tiles.

3. "Public's Policy Priorities Reflect Changing Conditions at Home and Abroad," Pew Research Center, January 15, 2015, http://www.people-press.org/2015/01/15/publics-policy-priorities-reflect-changing-conditions-at-home-and-abroad/#views-of-importance-of-environmental-protection-global-warming.

4. Ibid.

5. Ibid.

6. Barna Group, OmniPoll™ 1-12OL, national survey of 1,005 adults, conducted January 2012.

7. "Public's Policy Priorities," Pew Research Center.

8. Ibid.

9. Ibid.

10. Ibid.

11. "Most Important Problem," Gallup.

12. Barna Group, OmniPoll™ 1-12OL, national survey of 1,005 adults, conducted January 2012.

13. Kaye Foley, "America's Crumbling Infrastructure," Yahoo News, last accessed February 22, 2016, http://news.yahoo.com/america-s-crumbling-infrastructure-katie-couric-explains-170349892.html; *2013 Report Card for America's Infrastructure*, American Society of Civil Engineers, March 2013, http://www.infrastructurereportcard.org/wp-content/uploads/2013ReportCardforAmericasInfrastructure.pdf.

14. *Report Card*, American Society of Civil Engineers.

Chapter 12 Population Growth

1. "Demography of the United States," *Wikipedia*, last accessed January 21, 2016, https://en.wikipedia.org/wiki/Demographics_of_the_United_States; Joyce A. Martin, Brady E. Hamilton, and Michelle J.K. Osterman, "Births in the United States, 2014," NCHS Data Brief, no. 216 (Hyattsville, MD: National Center for Health Statistics, September 2015), http://www.cdc.gov/nchs/data/databriefs/db216.htm; http://www.cdc.gov/nchs/births.htm; "World Population: Major Trends," last accessed February 4, 2016, http://dwb4.unl.edu/Chem/CHEM869A/CHEM869ALinks/www.iiasa.ac.at/Research/LUC/Papers/gkh1/chap1.htm; Pew Research Center, "Chapter 1: Main Factors Driving Population Growth," *The Future of World Religions: Population Growth Projections, 2010–2050*, April 2, 2015, http://www.pewforum.org/2015/04/02/main-factors-driving-population-growth/.

2. "Demography," *Wikipedia*.

3. Wm. Robert Johnston, "Historical Abortion Statistics, United States," September 13, 2015, accessed January 21, 2016, http://www.johnstonsarchive.net/policy/abortion/ab-unitedstates.html.

4. Martin, Hamilton, and Osterman, "Births"; "Birth Data," Centers for Disease Control and Prevention, accessed January 21, 2016, http://www.cdc.gov/nchs/births.htm; Jones, "Voter Engagement;" "Major Trends," http://dwb4.unl.edu/Chem/CHEM869A/CHEM869ALinks/www.iiasa.ac.at/Research/LUC/Papers/gkh1/chap1.htm; Pew, "Chapter 1"; Pew Research Center, *The Future of World Religions: Population Growth Projections, 2010–2050*, April 2, 2015, http://www.pewforum.org/files/2015/03/PF_15.04.02_ProjectionsFullReport.pdf; Sandra L Colby and Jennifer M. Ortman, *Projections of the Size and Composition of the US Population: 2014 to 2060*, Current Population Reports, P25–1143, US Census Bureau, Washington, DC, 2014, http://www.census.gov/content/dam/Census/library/publications/2015/demo/p25-1143.pdf; *Statistical Abstract of the United States, 2012-2013*, 131st ed. (New York: Skyhorse Publishing, 2012), 77.

5. Pew, "Chapter 1"; Pew, *Future of World Religions*.

6. Johnston, "Historical Abortion Statistics"; *Statistical Abstract*, 836–38.

7. "Immigration to the United States," *Wikipedia*, last accessed January 29, 2016, https://en.wikipedia.org/wiki/Immigration_to_the_United_States; Jie Zong and Jeanne Batalova,

"Frequently Requested Statistics on Immigrants and Immigration in the United States," Migration Policy Institute, February 26, 2015, http://www.migrationpolicy.org/article /frequently-requested-statistics-immigrants-and-immigration-united-states/.

8. Colby and Ortman, *Size and Composition of the US Population,* Report P25-1143, March 3, 2015, https://www.census.gov/library/publications/2015/demo/p25-1143.html.

9. Various sociologists use different endpoints and labels for the generations they study. One of the more popular definitions indicate that Millennials—also called Generation Y, Digitals, or the Echo Boom—comprise the generation born from 1981–1997; Gen X or the Baby Busters were born from 1965–1980; the Baby Boom was 1946–1964; and the oldest Americans were born prior to 1946, going by a wide variety of names such as the Silent, Greatest, Senior, Elder, GI, Lost, and Mature Generation.

10. Richard Fry, "This Year Millennials Will Overtake Baby Boomers," Pew Research Center, January 16, 2015, http://www.pewresearch.org/fact-tank/2015/01/16/this-year-millennials -will-overtake-baby-boomers/; "2014 National Populations Projections: Summary Tables," Table 6, US Census Bureau, last accessed January 29, 2016, http://www.census.gov/population /projections/data/national/2014/summarytables.html.

11. *Statistical Abstract,* 8–9; "US and World Population Clock," last accessed January 29, 2016, http://www.census.gov/popclock/.

12. The estimate of births is from Johnston, "Historical Abortion Statistics." The estimate of deaths is from Centers for Disease Control and Prevention, "Death and Mortality," FastStats, last accessed February 4, 2016, http://www.cdc.gov/nchs/fastats/deaths.htm.

13. Pew, "Chapter 1," and Pew, "Future of World Religions."

14. Johnston, "Historical Abortion Statistics."

15. "Immigration," *Wikipedia*; Zong and Batalova, "Frequently Requested Statistics."

16. "Populations Projections," US Census Bureau.

Chapter 13 Happiness

1. The studies examined were conducted by Gallup Organization, Ipsos, Pew Research Center, Harris Interactive, Gallup International Association and WIN, National Institutes of Health, AARP, NORC, OECD, Bill and Melinda Gates Foundation, and UConn Poll.

2. "The Perfect Salary for Happiness: $75,000," Robert Frank, Wall Street Journal, September 7, 2010, http://blogs.wsj.com/wealth/2010/09/07/the-perfect-salary-for-happiness-75000 -a-year/; "At What Price Happiness? $75,000," Courtney Rubin, Inc., September 7, 2010, http://www.inc.com/news/articles/2010/09/study-says-$75,000-can-buy-happiness.html.

3. Harris Interactive national survey, fielded April 2013, N=2,345 adults 18 or older.

4. Gallup International Association, national survey conducted in December 2014, N=1,016; Harris Interactive survey conducted April 2013, N=2,345 adults; Heart & Mind Strategies, national survey conducted June 2012, N=4,397; General Social Survey, conducted by NORC, annual survey.

5. "Gallup Daily: US Mood tracking," Gallup, last accessed February 4, 2016, http:// www.gallup.com/poll/106915/Gallup-Daily-US-Mood.aspx.

6. "Beyond Happiness: Thriving," *AARP*, June 4, 2012, http://www.aarp.org/research /topics/life/info-2014/happiness-report-2012.html.

7. John 15:1–17; Rom. 4:8; 2 Cor. 6:3–10; Gal. 5:22.

Chapter 14 Life Satisfaction

1. Angus Deaton, "Income, Health, and Well-Being around the World," Journal of Economic Perspectives 22, no. 2 (Spring 2008). Also see Katie Simmons, "When It Comes

to Happiness, Money Matters," Pew Research Center, October 30, 2014, http://www.pew
research.org/fact-tank/2014/10/30/when-it-comes-to-happiness-money-matters/.

2. Kim Painter, "USA is Twelfth, Panama First, in Global Well-Being Poll," *USA Today*,
September 16, 2014, http://www.usatoday.com/story/news/nation/2014/09/16/global-well
-being-poll-panama/15679637/.

Chapter 15 Success

1. Accenture, "Accenture Research Finds Most Professionals Believe They Can 'Have
It All,'" news release, March 1, 2013, https://newsroom.accenture.com/subjects/corporate
-citizenship-philanthropy/accenture-research-finds-most-professionals-believe-they-can-have
-it-all. Based on a national survey conducted by Ipsos, for Strayer University, N=2,011, in
2014; Jacquelyn Smith, "This Is How Americans Define Success," *Business Insider*, October
3, 2014, http://www.businessinsider.com/how-americans-now-define-success-2014-10#ixzz3
g0D4jyvT; "Enjoy Life, Live with Parents: Millennials Redefine Adulthood," Science Codex,
July 30, 2014, http://www.sciencecodex.com/enjoy_life_live_with_parents_millennials
_redefine_adulthood-138600#ixzz3g0JesUBB; *Heartland Monitor Poll XIV*, Allstate/Na-
tional Journal, https://www.allstate.com/resources/Allstate/attachments/heartland-monitor
/heartland-XIV-data.pdf.

2. Jonah Lehrer, "Which Traits Predict Success? (The Importance of Grit)," *Wired*, March
14, 2011, http://www.wired.com/2011/03/what-is-success-true-grit/; "Gallup: The Six College
Experiences Linked to Lifelong Success," Education Advisory Board, April 9, 2015, https://
www.eab.com/daily-briefing/2015/04/09/gallup-life-success-linked-to-6-college-experiences.

3. Accenture, "Accenture Research."

4. "Family and Personal Accomplishments Lead People's List of Success Determinants,"
Barna Group, November 6, 2002, https://barna.org/component/content/article/5-barna
-update/45-barna-update-sp-657/84-family-and-personal-accomplishments-lead-peoples
-list-of-success-determinants#.Vqu_tvkrJD9.

5. Based on a national survey conducted by Ipsos, for Strayer University, N=2,011, in
2014; Smith, "How Americans Define Success."

6. National survey conducted among professionals by Accenture; Vicki Salemi, "New
Survey Defines Success on International Women's Day," *FishbowlNY*, March 8, 2013, http://
www.adweek.com/fishbowlny/new-survey-defines-success-on-international-womens-day
/322626.

7. Ibid.

8. Smith, "How Americans Define Success."

9. Accenture, "Accenture Research."

10. 1 Sam. 15:22; Col. 3:23.

Chapter 16 Morality

1. Based on research by the Barna Group, Ventura, CA, including OmniPoll 2-03, N=1,024,
conducted September 2003; OmniPoll Frames, N=1,005, conducted June 2013; and Omni-
Poll 1-14, N=1,024, conducted February 2014. Also based upon studies conducted by the
Gallup Organization, Princeton, NJ. Their related studies were conducted in May 2005
(N=1,005) and May 2015 (N=1,024). The data can be accessed at: http://www.gallup.com
/poll/16318/societys-moral-boundaries-expand-somewhat-year.aspx; and http://www.gallup
.com/poll/183413/americans-continue-shift-left-key-moral-issues.aspx.

2. Ibid.

3. Based on research by the Barna Group, Ventura, CA, including OmniPoll 2-03, N=1,024, conducted September 2003; OmniPoll Frames, N=1,005, conducted June 2013; OmniPoll 1-14, N=1,024, conducted February 2014.

4. Based on research by the Barna Group, Ventura, CA. Studies used include OmniPoll™ 2-03, N=1,024, conducted September 2003; Frames, N=1,005, conducted June 2013.

5. Gallup Organization surveys from 2005 and 2015, accessed from www.gallup.com /poll/1681/moral-issues.aspx.

6. Lydia Saad, "Government Named Top US Problem for Second Straight Year," Gallup, January 4, 2016, http://www.gallup.com/poll/187979/government-named-top-problem-second -straight-year.aspx?g_source=biggest%20problem&g_medium=search&g_campaign=tiles.

Chapter 17 Political Correctness

1. Bob Unruh, "Obama Signs 'End to Free Speech,'" WND, March 12, 2012, http://www .wnd.com/2012/03/obama-signs-end-to-free-speech/.

2. Napp Nazworth, "Liberals Become Dark, Cultish, Intellectually Stifling, Dissident Liberals Complain," *Christian Post*, May 20, 2015, http://www.christianpost.com/news /liberals-became-dark-cultish-intellectually-stifling-dissident-liberals-complain-136063/.

3. Zachary Leshin, "Dershowitz: 'The Fog of Fascism Is Descending Quickly over Many Universities,'" CNS news, November 13, 2015, http://www.cnsnews.com/blog/zachary-leshin /dershowitz-fog-fascism-descending-quickly-over-many-american-universities.

4. Charles Passy, "Deleted Tweet from Chick-fil-A Head Calls Gay Ruling 'Sad Day,'" *The Wall Street Journal*, June 26, 2013, http://blogs.wsj.com/speakeasy/2013/06/26/deleted -tweet-from-chick-fil-a-head-calls-same-sex-ruling-sad-day/.

5. "The Johns Hopkins Chick-fil-A Ban and the Coming Gay-Marriage Witch Hunt," Andrew Guernsey, *The National Review*, April 22, 2015, http://www.nationalreview.com /article/417305/sandwiches-repression-andrew-guernsey.

6. Catherine Rampell, "Free Speech Is Flunking Out on College Campuses," *Washington Post*, October 22, 2015, https://www.washingtonpost.com/opinions/free-speech-is-flunking -out-on-college-campuses/2015/10/22/124e7cd2-78f5-11e5-b9c1-f03c48c96ac2_story.html.

7. "Campus Speech Cops Ban 'Politically Correct,'" *New York Post*, October 22, 2015, http://nypost.com/2015/10/22/campus-speech-cops-ban-politically-correct/.

8. Jonah Goldberg, "Campus Commotions Show We're Raising Fragile Kids," *National Review*, November 11, 2015, http://www.nationalreview.com/article/426853/yale-student -protest-safe-space-political-correctness. Also, Meghan Daum, "The Tantrums at Mizzou and Yale Reveal More than PC Problems," *Chicago Tribune*, November 12, 2015, http:// www.chicagotribune.com/news/opinion/commentary/ct-yale-mizzou-colleges-free-speech -daum-20151112-column.html.

9. "79% See Political Correctness As Serious Problem in America," Rasmussen Reports, November 2, 2011, http://www.rasmussenreports.com/public_content/lifestyle/general_life style/october_2011/79_see_political_correctness_as_serious_problem_in_america.

10. Pew Research Center, national survey conducted March 19–April 29, 2014, N=2,439, as part of their American Trends Panel.

11. National survey by Opinion Research Corporation, for CNN, conducted May 29–31, 2015, N=1,025.

Chapter 18 Confidence in Institutions

1. "Confidence in Institutions," Gallup Organization, last accessed February 2, 2016, http://www.gallup.com/poll/1597/Confidence-Institutions.aspx.

2. Ibid.

3. Ibid.

Chapter 19 Retirement

1. Barna Group, OmniPoll™ June 2013, a national survey of 1,005 adults, conducted June 2013.

2. D'Vera Cohn and Paul Taylor, "Baby Boomers Approach 65—Glumly," Pew Research Center, December 20, 2010, http://www.pewsocialtrends.org/2010/12/20/baby-boomers -approach-65-glumly/; "2014 National Populations Projections," US Census Bureau. Also, Loraine A. West, Samantha Cole, Daniel Goodkind, and Wan He, *65+ in the United States: 2010,* Current Population Report P23-212, US Census Bureau, issued June 2014.

3. Alicia H. Munnell, "The Average Retirement Age—An Update," *Issue in Brief,* no. 15-4 (March 2015), http://crr.bc.edu/wp-content/uploads/2015/03/IB_15-4.pdf; Rebecca Riffkin, "Average US Retirement Age Rises to 62," April 28, 2014, http://www.gallup.com/poll/168707 /average-retirement-age-rises.aspx; "Average Retirement Age for Men, 1962–2012," Center for Retirement Research at Boston College, March 2013, http://crr.bc.edu/wp-content/up loads/1012/01/Avg_ret_age_men1.pdf.

4. Ruth Helman, Craig Copeland, and Jack VanDerhei, "The 2015 Retirement Confi- dence Survey: Having a Retirement Savings Plan a Key Factor in Americans' Retirement Confidence," *Issue Brief,* no. 413 (April 2015), http://www.ebri.org/pdf/surveys/rcs/2015 /EBRI_IB_413_Apr15_RCS-2015.pdf.

5. Barna Group, Frames W3, national survey of 1,000 adults, conducted August 2013.

6. Barna Group, OmniPoll™ June 2013, a national survey of 1,005 adults, conducted June 2013; Barna Group, Frames W3, national survey of 1,000 adults, conducted August 2013.

7. Alicia H. Munnell, Anthony Webb, Luke Delorme, and Francesca Golub-Sass, "Na- tional Retirement Risk Index: How Much Longer Do We Need to Work?" *Issue in Brief,* no. 12-12 (June 2012), http://crr.bc.edu/wp-content/uploads/2012/06/IB_12-12-508.pdf.

8. Matthew Heimer, "Charts Show Who's Not Saving for Retirement," Market Watch, March 21, 2014, http://blogs.marketwatch.com/encore/2014/03/21/chart-shows-whos-saving -for-retirement-whos-not/; Alicia H. Munnell, "Dismal Fed Data on Retirement Saving," Market Watch, September 18, 2014, http://blogs.marketwatch.com/encore/2014/09/18 /dismal-fed-data-on-retirement-saving/.

9. Robert Laura, "Average Americans May Never Retire, but That's Okay," *Forbes,* Oc- tober 24, 2015, http://www.forbes.com/sites/robertlaura/2015/10/24/average-americans-may -never-retire-but-thats-okay/?ss=retirement.

10. Ibid.; "Average Retirement Savings Statistics," Financial Freedom Advantage, last accessed February 24, 2016, http://www.financialfreedomadvantage.com/average-retirement -savings.html.

11. Emily Brandon, "The Baby Boom Retirement Crunch Begins," *US News & World Report,* May 13, 2013, http://money.usnews.com/money/retirement/articles/2013/05/13/the -baby-boomer-retirement-crunch-begins; "Ten Ways Baby Boomers Will Reinvent Retirement," *US News & World Report,* February 16, 2010, http://money.usnews.com/money/retirement /slideshows/10-ways-baby-boomers-will-reinvent-retirement.

12. Munnell, "Average Retirement"; Riffkin, "Average US Retirement Age"; "Retirement Age for Men," Center for Retirement Research at Boston College.

13. Helman, Copeland, and VanDerhei, "2015 Retirement Confidence Survey."

14. Ibid.

15. Ibid.

16. "2014 National Populations Projections," US Census Bureau.

17. "The Retirement Income Deficit," Retirement USA, last accessed February 3, 2016, http://www.retirement-usa.org/retirement-income-deficit-0.

18. Laura, "Americans May Never Retire."

19. Ronald Brownstein, "A Glass Half (uh, Two-Thirds) Empty," *National Journal*, October 7, 2015, http://www.nationaljournal.com/next-economy/tk.

Chapter 20 The Future

1. "New The Atlantic/Aspen Institute Survey: Majority of Americans Express Optimism About Own Lives, yet Believe American Dream Is Suffering," PR Newswire, July 1, 2015, http://www.prnewswire.com/news-releases/new-the-atlanticaspen-institute-survey-majority-of-americans-express-optimism-about-own-lives-yet-believe-american-dream-is-suffering-300107748.html.

2. "The Sky Is Falling (and the Boogeyman Is Chasing Me)," Wilkinson College of Arts, Humanities, and Social Sciences, October 21, 2014, https://blogs.chapman.edu/wilkinson/2014/10/21/the-sky-is-falling-and-the-boogeyman-is-chasing-me/.

3. Ipsos, "Consumer Reinvention Uncovers Potential Opportunities for Unmet Needs," Ipsos, news release, June 11, 2015, http://www.ipsos-na.com/news-polls/pressrelease.aspx?id=6883.

4. "New The Atlantic/Aspen Institute Survey," *PR Newswire*.

5. Ibid.

6. CNN/ORC Poll. Fieldwork conducted May 29–June 1, 2014. N=1,003 adults nationwide.

7. NBC News/Wall Street Journal Poll conducted by Peter Hart & Associates and by Public Opinion Strategies. Fieldwork conducted April 23–27, 2014. N=500 adults nationwide.

8. Ibid.

9. CNN/ORC Poll. Fieldwork conducted May 29–June 1, 2014. N=1,003 adults nationwide.

10. Ipsos, "Consumer Reinvention."

11. George Barna and David Barton, *U-Turn: Restoring America to the Strength of Its Roots* (Lake Mary: FL: Frontline, 2014), 8–24.

Chapter 21 What You Can Do

1. A comprehensive discussion of vision, vision development, and the implementation of vision is contained in my book *The Power of Vision* (Grand Rapids: Baker Books, 1992).

2. Paul Sabatier, *Life of St. Francis of Assisi* (C Scribner's Sons, 1894), xi–xii.

3. Much of the content in this section of the chapter is based on a series of blog posts that originally appeared at my website (Georgebarna.com). Those posts have been edited and updated to fit this context.

4. Statistics such as those who are saved, or those who have been broken, are our best estimates of how many people fit those conditions. Only God truly knows how many people meet His qualifications; the survey data are merely an approximation using the best human tools available. Such characterizations are not an effort to judge people but to give those who wish to solve problems related to estimates a sense of how serious a problem may be.

5. The data in this section of the chapter are largely drawn from the research contained in my book *Maximum Faith: Live Like Jesus* and from several recent national surveys by Metaformation, American Culture & Faith Institute, and the Barna Group that have explored facets of people's transformational journey.

6. My book on worldview development is *Think Like Jesus*. Others to consider include *How Now Shall We Live* by Charles Colson and Nancy Pearcey; *Total Truth* by Nancy

Pearcey; *Understanding the Times* by Dr. Jenn Meyers and David Noebel; *All Truth Is God's Truth* by Arthur Holmes; *A Christian Manifesto* by Francis Schaeffer; and *Building a Christian Worldview* by W. Andrew Hoffecker and Gary Scott Smith.

7. These statistics are drawn from a series of studies by the Barna Group among national random samples of adults eighteen and older, with each study including a minimum of one thousand respondents.

George Barna has filled executive roles in politics, marketing, advertising, media development, research, and ministry. He founded the Barna Research Group in 1984 (now the Barna Group) and helped it become a leading marketing research firm focused on the intersection of faith and culture before selling it in 2009. Through the Barna Group, George has served several hundred parachurch ministries, thousands of Christian churches, and many other nonprofit and for-profit organizations, as well as the US military.

He currently serves as the executive director of the American Culture & Faith Institute (a division of United in Purpose) and is president of Metaformation, a faith development organization. He also has served as a pollster to candidates in three presidential campaigns.

Barna has written more than fifty books, mostly addressing cultural trends, leadership, spiritual development, and church dynamics. They include *New York Times* bestsellers and several award-winning books. His works have been translated into more than a dozen foreign languages. He has sold more books based on survey research related to matters of faith than any author in American history.

His work is frequently cited as an authoritative source by the media. Barna has been hailed as "the most quoted person in the Christian Church today" and has been named by various media as one of the nation's most influential Christian leaders.

A frequent speaker at ministry conferences around the world, he has been on the faculty at several universities and seminaries. He also has helped to start several churches and has served as a pastor of a large, multiethnic church, as well as the leader of a house church.

After graduating summa cum laude from Boston College, Barna earned two master's degrees from Rutgers University and a doctorate from Dallas Baptist University.

George and his wife, Nancy, attended high school and college together before marrying in 1978. They have three adopted daughters and one grandchild, live on the central California coast, and attend Mission Church in Ventura. He enjoys reading, listening to music, rooting for the Yankees and Lakers, and relaxing on the beach.

The American Culture & Faith Institute is committed to providing ongoing research about the opinions, attitudes, values, beliefs, and behaviors of spiritually active Christians who are attentive to politics and government and have a theologically and politically conservative worldview. This group—named SAGE Cons, an acrostic for Spiritually Active, Governance Engaged Conservatives—has historically had significant influence on the course of America and has the capacity to continue to exert such influence.

ACFI conducts regular national studies among SAGE Cons and reports the findings. ACFI also regularly tracks the thinking and actions of theologically conservative pastors. Led by researcher George Barna, ACFI is the only organization that has developed a longitudinal study of SAGE Cons and of theologically conservative pastors.

You can have access to the research findings at:
www.CultureFaith.com

At that website you can also:

- Sign up for ACFI's free e-newsletter, *SAGE Con Weekly*
- Access groundbreaking national research reports examining faith, politics, and cultural transformation
- View weekly statistical updates on the opinions and behavior of conservative Christians

ACFI is a division of United in Purpose, a nonpartisan, not-for-profit organization. United in Purpose is committed to educating, motivating, and activating the body of Christ to work together toward transforming the culture in ways that are consistent with the Scriptures and honor God.

www.CultureFaith.com

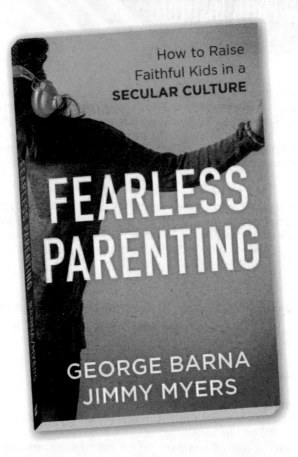